D0125113

# SEX:
## A USER'S
## MANUAL

THE DIAGRAM
GROUP

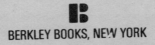

BERKLEY BOOKS, NEW YORK

This Berkley book contains the complete
text of the original hardcover edition.
It has been completely reset in a typeface
designed for easy reading and was printed
from new film.

SEX: A USER'S MANUAL

A Berkley Book / published by arrangement with
the author

PRINTING HISTORY
G. P. Putnam's Sons edition / July 1981
Berkley edition / June 1982

ISBN: 0-425-08972-X

A BERKLEY BOOK ® TM 757,375
Berkley Books are published by The Berkley Publishing Group,
200 Madison Avenue, New York, NY 10016.
The name "BERKLEY" and the "B" logo
are trademarks belonging to Berkley Publishing Corporation.

PRINTED IN THE UNITED STATES OF AMERICA

20   19   18   17

# The Diagram Group

**Managing editor**      Ruth Midgley

**Research editor**      Norma Jack

**Contributors**      Ann Kramer
David Lambert

**Picture researcher**      Enid Moore
**Indexer**      Mary Ling

**Art director**      Kathleen McDougall

**Art editor**      Mark Evans

**Artists**      Steven Clark
Stephen Gyapay
Brian Hewson
Richard Hummerstone
Janos Marffy
Graham Rosewarne
**Art assistant**      Sean Gilbert

**Consultants**      Toni Belfield
Medical Information Officer
Family Planning Information Service
D.B. Garrioch, MD, MRCOG
Senior Registrar in Gynaecology
St Thomas' Hospital, London

**Acknowledgment**      The authors and editors of the Diagram
Group here wish to acknowledge their debt
to the many individuals and institutions
whose detailed research projects into sexual
topics have provided data for diagrams in
this book.
If we have unwittingly infringed copyright
in any way, we tender our sincere apologies
and will be glad of the opportunity, upon
being satisfied as to the owner's title, to pay
an appropriate fee as if we had been able to
obtain prior permission.

Frontispiece by C.L. Desrais to
*Le petit-neveu de Boccace,*
published in France in 1781.

# Foreword

The twentieth century has seen enormous changes in our knowledge and attitudes about sex. This book could not have been published in earlier times. It includes the most up-to-date information on every aspect of the human sexual experience, and by its clear presentation and ready accessibility to the general reader it aims to dispel the many deep fears and prejudices that a discussion of sexual topics all too often arouses.

Current literature on sex and sexuality tends to fall into one of two categories. It is either coldly clinical and full of technical terms, or it is titillating and more or less blatantly pornographic. In each case the general reader is likely to be inhibited by the way in which information is presented. **Sex: A User's Manual** represents a new departure in this respect. It is the first really straightforward visual guide to all aspects of human sexuality. The clear, concise text is scientifically correct but easy to understand. The style of illustration, too, has been chosen with care. It is non-technical but accurate, explicit but non-pornographic, and makes imaginative use of diagrams to bring statistical information to life.

Recent years have seen a great deal of serious research into a wide variety of sexual topics, but the results of these researches are not always easily accessible to the general public. **Sex: A User's Manual** seeks to summarize current information about sex and sexuality and to present this information in an interesting and easy-to-follow manner. Its popular approach will, we hope, make it an invaluable reference volume, providing every reader with answers to his or her own many questions on this most fascinating of subjects.

# Contents

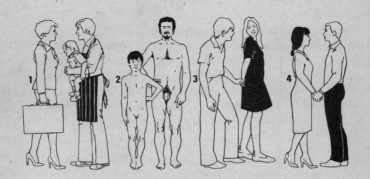

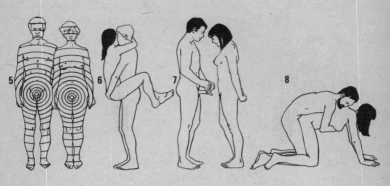

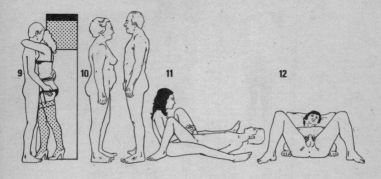

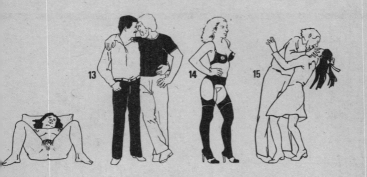

# Chapter 1

1 Card advertising a Chinese brothel, 1920s.
2,4 Advertisements from the Sears, Roebuck catalogue, 1908.
3 Romantic book illustration, English, 1860s.
5 Selecting a prostitute, from a German book of c. 1910.

3

1

秦皇島海陽路

玉貞班

### YUH CHEN PAN

### No. 1 WHORE HOUSE

HAE YANG LU

CHIN WANG TAO

4

### Genuine O. P. C. Suspensory.

This is the one to buy. This Genuine O. P. C. Suspensory should be worn by every healthy normal man. The vital organs need a suspensory to sustain the nervous vitality, energy and force and prevent strain.

2

### Famous H. & H. Bust Forms.
The only bust form made which defies detection.

Nature's Only Rival.

The celebrated H. & H. Bust Forms are now so perfect that they cannot be detected from the natural bust, whether by sight or touch. Strikingly stylish, a source of relief, delight and pride to the wearer and of admiration to others. Very durable, economic and hygienic. These forms do away with all unsightly, unhealthy and uncomfortable padding. They produce perfectly the full bust and slender waist decreed by the latest fashion. Positively the only device which perfectly simulates flesh and blood. Applied in an instant; made of white rubber, invisible with any costume; neither sight nor touch reveals their use.

5

# Sexual patterns 1

**Popular movements**

Present-day sexual behavior has been considerably affected by the emergence of various popular socio-political movements. Among the most far-reaching of these have been the "youth culture" of the 1960s, the Feminist Movement, and Gay Liberation. All three have questioned and challenged sexual stereotypes and traditional sexual values.

**Sex in the open**

Sex today is truly out in the open. Explicit sexuality and eroticism are increasingly seen in all forms of entertainment — in theater, cinema, television, and magazines. Modern advertising makes much use of sexual imagery as an incentive to buy, while sexual aids and commodities themselves have probably never been so widely available.

14

# Sex and society

Sex influences our whole lives. At its most basic, sex is a question of gender, whether we are male or female. This primary distinction into two sexes provides the human species with its means of reproduction. But its influence extends far beyond the range of sexual activity. Every aspect of our personal, social and cultural lives is to some extent affected by our gender.

While general patterns of sexual activity, in terms of who does what to whom, have probably changed very little in the course of Western history, attitudes toward sexual behavior have changed a great deal. One of the most striking changes in recent times has been the acceptance of sex as a valid expression of intimacy and a source of pleasure divorced from procreation. Another major change is that sex is now out in the open. Probably never before has sex been so openly displayed and publicly discussed as it is today. At the same time, sex and sexuality are being redefined and reevaluated so that the range of acceptable sexual expression is expanding. Some of the old taboos are disappearing, and previously unacceptable aspects of sexual behavior are now being accepted and incorporated into the general culture.

# Sexual patterns 2

## Clothing and sexuality

Clothes are a very obvious demonstration of shifting social attitudes. Less than 100 years ago not only most of the human body but also sometimes piano and table legs were expected to be modestly covered. Today, Western fashion either emphasizes sexuality or, in the case of "unisex" styles, plays down the differences between the sexes.

## Changing social roles

Stereotyped sexual role casting is currently being challenged. Increasing numbers of women are now in employment, deliberately rejecting the social role that made them purely wife and mother. Men are now more likely to join in domestic activities and child-rearing, and also to question traditionally held male views about the status of women.

# Sex and society

## A valid form of intimacy

Wide acceptance of birth control and the advent of the pill have encouraged the acceptance of sex as a valid form of intimacy and a source of pleasure. Premarital sex and non-marital cohabitation are now commonly accepted. The new sexual awareness has also led to a challenging of the "double standard" of morality that permitted greater freedom to men.

## A greater understanding

Past decades have seen a huge increase in knowledge about sex and sexuality. Major research landmarks include the work of Alfred Kinsey in the 1940s and of Masters and Johnson in the 1960s. Greater understanding about the importance of sexuality in human development and relationships is now evident in sex education and in the practice of sex therapy.

© DIAGRAM

# Survey of attitudes 1

In recent years there has been a great deal of talk and publicity about the so-called sexual revolution and its accompanying permissive society. Certainly there have been some real and major changes within Western society as a whole, but the extent to which this so-called revolution has changed people's individual behavior and basic sexual attitudes is still highly debatable.

In 1977 *Time* magazine commissioned a survey of American views on sexual morality, some of the results of which are included on these pages. While acknowledging the problem of determining the truthfulness of people's replies when questioned on sexual topics, the *Time* report produced some interesting conclusions. A majority of Americans (68% of those polled) apparently feel that it is a good thing to have more openness about things like sex, homosexuality, and premarital and extramarital relations. But acceptance of the so-called "new morality" is by no means absolute. As individual answers showed, there is still strong support for the traditional institutions of marriage and family, and the conflict between old and new ideas on sexual morality was found to have produced a state of "moral confusion" in 61% of the people polled.

# Sex and society

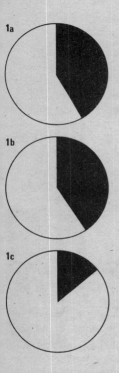

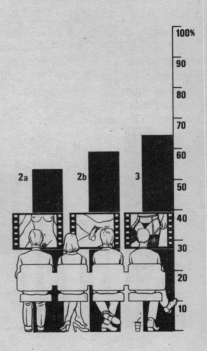

## Survey of attitudes

Data here is taken from a 1977 poll by Yankelovich, Skelly & White of 1044 US *Time* magazine readers from different regional, racial, age and religious groups.

**1 Attitudes over last few years**

**a** 42% reported no change.

**b** 41% said they had become more liberal.

**c** 15% said they had become more conservative.

## 2 Nudity in movies

**a** Female nudity in movies was disapproved of by 54% of the people asked.

**b** Male nudity in movies, which is comparatively less common, was disapproved of by 59% of the survey's respondents.

## 3 Pornographic movies

Pornography in movies was thought to be morally wrong by 64% of the people asked.

©DIAGRAM

19

# Survey of attitudes 2

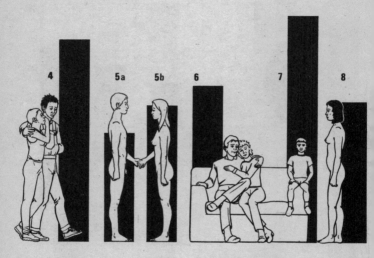

**4 Teenage sex**
Sexual relations between teenagers were disapproved of by 63% of all people asked, but only by 34% of respondents aged under 25 years.

**5 Premarital sex**
**a** Only 34% thought it was wrong for a man to have intercourse before marriage.
**b** But 42% thought a woman should not have premarital sex.

**6 Cohabitation**
Fewer than half of the people asked — 48% — did not agree that it was morally acceptable for a couple to live together before marriage.

**7 Children outside marriage**
Having children without formal marriage was disapproved of by 70% of respondents.

**8 Abortion**
Abortion was considered morally wrong by 44% of those asked (48% thought it acceptable and 8% did not know).

**9 Infidelity**
**a** Infidelity by a married man was considered morally wrong by 76% of respondents.
**b** But 79% disapproved of infidelity by a married woman.

**10 Partner swapping**
This was disapproved of more strongly than other forms of infidelity: 81% considered partner-swapping morally wrong.

**11 Homosexuality**
Homosexual activity between consenting adults was thought to be morally wrong by 47% of those asked (43% thought it acceptable; 10% did not know).

©DIAGRAM

# Marriage 1

Basically marriage is a social and legal contract. In the past it often had very little to do with love or any other emotional considerations. It was a purely practical proposition, often arranged by the couple's families, and was the only socially acceptable way in which a couple could express their sexuality and become parents.

Today many of the traditional reasons for marriage are no longer universally accepted. Most people are now free to choose their own partners. Sex before marriage has become the rule rather than the exception, and increasing numbers of couples are choosing not to go through a marriage ceremony at all, but to live together and maybe even to bring up children without marriage.

Despite these changes and despite an evident reduction in annual marriage rates in many countries, the great majority of adults still choose to conduct their adult lives within the traditional social framework that marriage provides. In the United States, for example, it has been estimated that nine out of ten people will marry at least once by the time they are fifty. And although many more marriages now end in divorce, the majority of divorcees soon remarry.

People marry for a great many reasons — some practical and some emotional. To many couples marriage represents a public expression of a personal commitment based on mutual love. Others marry in an attempt to find emotional or financial security, perhaps using marriage as a means of escape from loneliness or an unhappy family background. The desire to start a family within a legally structured framework is another common reason for marriage. Despite the difficulties involved, the hope of creating a mutually happy and fulfilling relationship within a legally sanctioned marriage remains one of the most compelling social forces of our time.

# Sex and society

Men

Women

## Single or married

This diagram, based on US Government statistics, shows percentages of US men and women, born between 1900 and 1959, who in 1975 were single or had ever been married.

**a** Single 26.1% men, 20.6% women.

**b** Ever married once 62.5% men, 67% women.

**c** Ever married twice or more 11.3% men, 12.4% women.

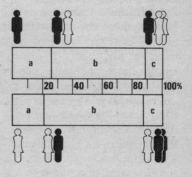

## Age at first marriage

Here we compare the median ages of men and women marrying for the first time in 1975.

**A** In the USA, where couples typically marry quite young, the median age for men was 22.7 years and for women 20.8 years.

**B** In the UK first marriages tend to occur later, the median age for men being 24.9 years and for women 22.7 years.

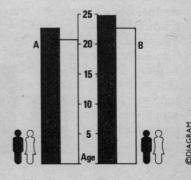

©DIAGRAM

23

# Marriage 2

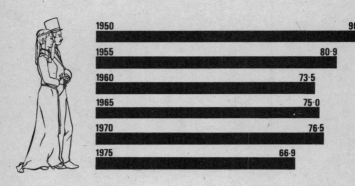

| Year | |
|---|---|
| 1950 | 90·2 |
| 1955 | 80·9 |
| 1960 | 73·5 |
| 1965 | 75·0 |
| 1970 | 76·5 |
| 1975 | 66·9 |

**Falling marriage rate** (*above*)
In 1975 some 2,153,000 US couples entered into marriage. This compares with 1,667,000 in 1950. There was, however, a fall in the rate of brides' first marriages during this 25-year period. Our diagram shows for different years the number of brides' first marriages for every 1000 single women aged 14 years and over.

**Increase in remarriage** (*below*)
Remarriage showed a great rise in popularity in the USA in the 15 years from 1960-75. Our diagram on remarriage compares actual numbers of brides aged 14 years and over who remarried in different years.
**A** 197,000 in 1960.
**B** 305,000 in 1965.
**C** 393,000 in 1970.
**D** 510,000 in 1975.

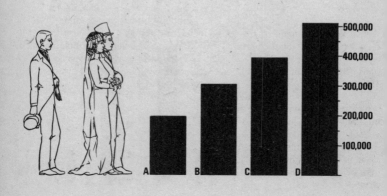

  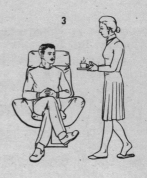

## Marriage patterns

A study by Cuber and Harroff of middle-aged upper middle class couples in the USA showed the following five distinct marriage patterns. The first three in our list — with their serious deficiencies — were much more common than the final two. It seems very likely that findings would be similar for people of other classes and nationalities.

**1** A controlled conflict marriage in which conflict and tensions are present but where outward hostility is avoided.

**2** A devitalized marriage that is predominantly based on habit but in which there is little actual conflict.

**3** A passively content marriage in which the partners believe themselves contented but where zest and vitality are lacking.

**4** A vital marriage in which the couple share a positive interest such as children, work, or a leisure activity.

**5** A total marriage in which the partners share a wide range of interests both inside and outside the home.

© DIAGRAM

# Divorce 1

Most couples enter marriage with the thought that it will last for ever. But in practice many marriages do break down and some break down irretrievably.

Marriages run into difficulties for many reasons. These may include basic incompatibility, sexual problems, the arrival of children and related stresses, infidelity, the onset of middle age, and the failure of one partner to adapt to the other's needs or changes. Increased life expectancy, too, has placed a very fundamental strain on marriage today. A couple who marry young and finish raising their children early may still have half their adult lives to live, and in such cases emotional and sexual apathy and boredom can become real dangers. At the same time, the shift of emphasis in marriage from parenthood to partnership has placed a more subtle strain on marriage, so that failure to achieve an ideal relationship can result in damaging disillusionment and conflict. In fact, given the difficulties today of maintaining any sort of lifelong, sexually exclusive relationship, what is perhaps surprising is not that so many marriages fail but that so many manage to survive.

In the past, social pressures were such that most couples stayed together whatever their difficulties. Today, some couples continue living together under conditions that

many outsiders would consider intolerable, others are helped by counseling or therapy to resolve their problems, and others attempt living separately for a trial period. Once a marriage has irretrievably broken down, however, divorce provides a legal clarification of the couple's situation. Although increasing numbers are now seeking divorce, most divorcees marry again. Indeed it could be argued that divorce allows a more realistic view of marriage, and provides an acceptable compromise between traditional monogamy and the possibility of having more than one marriage partner.

## Marital breakdowns
Here we picture some common reasons for marital breakdown.
**1** General incompatibility of personalities, aims and interests causes many marriages to founder. Sometimes the problem is a result of marrying too early, before mature views are formed.
**2** Sexual problems can disrupt the relationship of even the most loving partners (see pp. 250-269).

**3** Money is a common cause of marital conflict. Perhaps the wife spends more than her husband can afford, or perhaps he spends too much money on himself.
**4** Conflicting demands of home and work also cause disharmony. Perhaps the husband spends too much time at work, or maybe she wants to work and he says no.
**5** Young children can put strain on a marriage. Maybe the wife is getting insufficient help, or perhaps the husband thinks his wife no longer cares about him.
**6** Drinking too heavily can be either a cause or a symptom of marital problems.
**7** Infidelity, too, often occurs when a marriage is already under pressure for other reasons.
**8** Cruelty, either physical or mental, can make it intolerable for a couple to stay together.

©DIAGRAM

# Divorce 2

**Duration of failed marriages**
Compared here are official US estimates, based on sample data, of the median duration of US marriages ending in divorce or annulment in selected years.

**a** 1950: 5.3 years.
**b** 1955: 6.2 years.
**c** 1960: 7.1 years.
**d** 1965: 7.2 years.
**e** 1970: 6.7 years.
**f** 1975: 6.5 years.

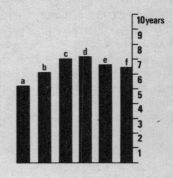

**Divorces and annulments**
Based on US Government figures, this diagram shows US divorces and annulments as a rate per 1000 married women aged 15 years and over. The figure for 1975 dramatically exceeds even the postwar high of 1945.

**A** 1925: 7.2
**B** 1935: 7.8
**C** 1945: 14.4
**D** 1955: 9.3
**E** 1965: 10.6
**F** 1975: 20.3

# Sex and society

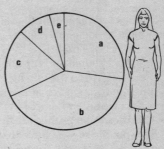

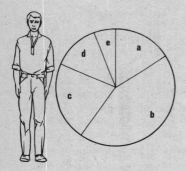

**Age at end of marriage** (*above*)
This diagram, based on official US estimates from sample data, shows the percentages of men (m) and women (w) in different age groups at the time of their divorces or annulments in 1975.
**a** Under 25yr: 16% (m), 27% (w).
**b** 25-34yr: 44% (m), 41% (w).
**c** 35-44yr: 22% (m), 19% (w).
**d** 45-54yr: 12% (m), 9% (w).
**e** 55 and over: 6% (m), 4% (w).

**Percentages divorced** (*below*)
Compared here are official US figures for percentages of divorcees among US males and females aged 18 years and over. As our diagram shows, the 1970s saw very marked increases.
**A** In 1950: 1.8% (m), 2.3% (w).
**B** In 1970: 2.5% (m), 3.9% (w).
**C** In 1973: 3.0% (m), 4.5% (w).
**D** In 1975: 4.0% (m), 5.3% (w).
**E** In 1977: 4.5% (m), 6.2% (w).

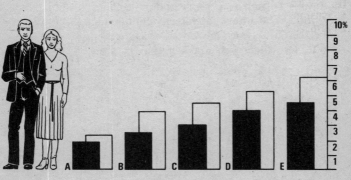

©DIAGRAM

# Sex and the law 1

Sex, like almost any other aspect of human behavior, is subject to social and legal controls. In most societies these controls have traditionally been based on two assumptions: first, that sexual activity should be directed toward procreation and the raising of offspring within stable family units, and second, that the human sex drive is a force with antisocial potential, making it necessary for certain activities to be prohibited by law.

Few people now believe that sexual activity should be restricted by law to the process of procreation — a view that finds its expression in the removal of legal sanctions against sexual activities between consenting adults in private. Even where there have been no changes in laws against such activities as sex outside marriage, non-coital sexual activity, homosexuality and even prostitution, there has been a marked relaxation in their enforcement. Liberalization of the law is also seen in the widespread reduction of penalties for public-nuisance type offenses such as exhibitionism and peeping, and also in the relaxation of laws against pornography.

Liberalization of sex laws in general is in no way inconsistent with retaining appropriate penalties for sexual activities — such as rape or child molestation — that continue to be almost universally condemned. What we have seen in the past few decades is a redefinition of what should realistically be considered a sex "crime."

### Sexual activity

Laws regulating sexual activity commonly lag behind current practices. In much of the USA, for example, oral sex, anal sex and in some states also mutual masturbation are illegal, even for married couples. Premarital sex and adultery, too, are often prohibited. Prosecutions are, however, unlikely, and there is growing pressure for reform.

### Contraception and abortion

Laws relating to birth control and abortion have undergone gradual liberalization. Few countries now operate laws that prohibit contraceptives, but availability and publicity vary considerably. Likewise abortion is now legal in most countries, but the grounds on which it is permitted and the limitations imposed vary a great deal.

©DIAGRAM

# Sex and the law 2

**Divorce**
Until the 1960s obtaining a divorce in the USA and in most European countries depended upon establishing one partner as "guilty" and the other as injured or innocent. Modern divorce laws mean that the question of guilt need no longer arise; the "irretrievable breakdown" of a marriage is now accepted as legal grounds for divorce.

**Homosexuality**
Homosexual activity between consenting adults in private was legalized in France as long ago as 1810. Other countries that now have similar laws include Sweden (1944), England and Wales (1967), Norway (1972) and Scotland (1980). In the USA, homosexuality itself is legal but homosexual acts still carry penalties in many states.

**Obscenity and pornography**
Laws relating to pornography are usually justified in terms of its possible, though unproved, effects, on children, morality and the incidence of sex crimes. Problems of defining what is pornographic have caused legal confusion in many countries. Also, the late 1970s saw something of a backlash after a decade of liberalization.

**Prostitution**
Despite being illegal in many countries, prostitution still flourishes. Recent years have seen campaigns for wider acceptance by prostitutes' collectives, notably in England and France. Soliciting, the usual charge against prostitutes, is the only sexual offense for which women are prosecuted to any significant degree.

© DIAGRAM

# Chapter 2

An unusual case for the doctor in this cartoon from a 1925 issue of the German satirical magazine *Simplicissimus*.

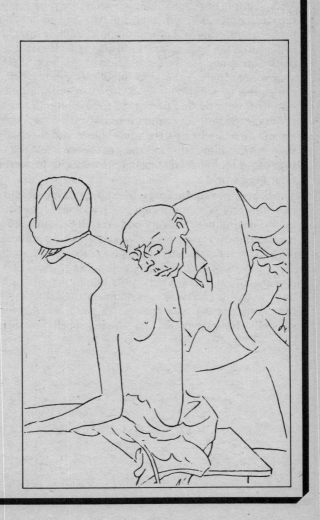

# Sex determination 1

Many simple one-celled animals are unisex: each one reproduces itself by splitting into two cells identical with their parent. Man and other complex animals breed differently. Such species contain males and females. Special cells from a male and a female fuse to produce a cell that shares hereditary material from both its parents. This cell multiplies by splitting to give rise to an adult organism identical with neither parent. So sexual reproduction produces countless permutations of individuals. This means there are likely to be some able to endure changes to their surroundings that kill most of the rest. Sex, then, is an ingenious biological device to help a species to survive in a changing world.

The blueprint determining which sex you are was laid down in your parents' chromosomes — packages of hereditary material contained in every body cell. By determining how each cell grows, your chromosomes also help control such hereditary traits as body build and color of hair and eyes. The nucleus of each ordinary cell holds 23 pairs of chromosomes. When a cell splits in two to build or repair body tissue its chromosomes double up and divide, so each new daughter cell also receives 23 pairs. But sperm (male sex cells) and eggs or ova (the female sex cells) are different.

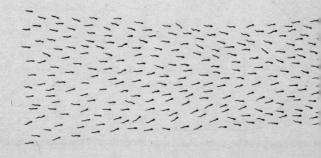

When the body makes sex cells each gets only 23 chromosomes, one of which carries a sex-determining factor. All eggs and one in two sperm have what is called an X chromosome, which carries the "female" factor. The other sperm have a Y chromosome carrying the "male" factor. If an egg is fertilized by a sperm with an X chromosome the resulting child will have two X chromosomes (XX) and be female. If fertilization is by a sperm with a Y chromosome, the child will have one X and one Y chromosome (XY) and be male.

Rare errors in the reassortment and recombination of chromosomes either during sex cell formation or fertilization result in chromosomal sex abnormalities, of which the following are examples. An XXX combination results in a normal-looking but possibly infertile female. If there is one X but no Y chromosome (X0), the result is an infertile female with sex organs that fail to mature. An XYY combination results in a male with normal sex organs, but perhaps with other problems. Combinations such as XXY or XXXYY produce males whose sex organs remain immature and who may develop female secondary sexual characteristics at puberty.

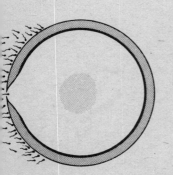

**Sperm and egg**
Male sex cells (sperm) are here shown to the same scale as a female sex cell (egg or ovum). Human sperm are about 0.05mm long, of which 0.045mm is tail. Human eggs measure about 1mm in diameter, making them about the size of a small pin head.

©DIAGRAM

# Sex determination 2

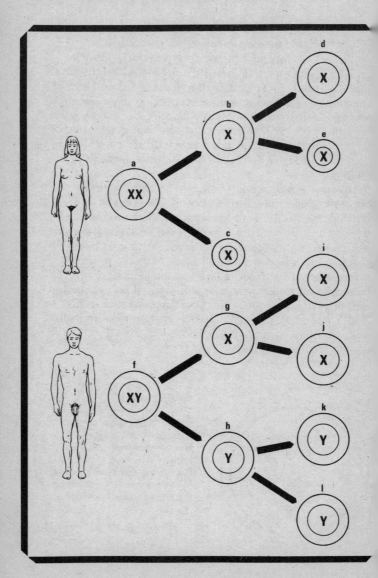

# Physiology of sex

**Sex chromosomes and eggs** (*left*)
Women's sex cells arise from so-called primary oocytes. The nucleus of a primary oocyte (**a**) includes a pair of X (female) sex chromosomes, so named for their shape. When the oocyte splits it gives a secondary oocyte (**b**) and a small, polar body (**c**). Each receives one X chromosome but only the secondary oocyte becomes a mature egg (**d**). Polar bodies (**c,e**) degenerate.

**Sex chromosomes and sperm**
Men's sex cells arise from primary spermatogonia. The nucleus of a primary spermatocyte (**f**) has an unmatched pair of sex cells: one X (female) and one Y (male). When the spermatocyte splits it gives rise to two secondary spermatocytes (**g,h**). One gets an X chromosome, the other a Y. When the secondary spermatocytes split one produces two X sperm (**i,j**); the other produces two Y sperm (**k,l**).

**A girl or a boy** (*below*)
An egg always has an X (female) chromosome. Sperm have either an X or a Y (male) chromosome. If an X sperm fertilizes an egg, the zygote (fertilized egg) gets one X chromosome from the egg and one from the sperm. An XX zygote grows into a girl (**1**). But if a Y sperm fertilizes the egg, the resulting zygote is XY, and grows into a boy (**2**).

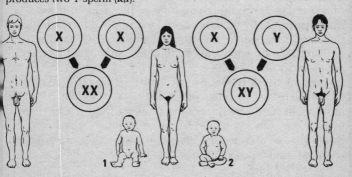

©DIAGRAM

39

# Preselecting gender 1

Until recently it was generally thought that chance alone determined a baby's gender, although superstition through the ages has spawned many supposed recipes for "getting a boy." The idea that it might be possible for a couple to preselect the sex of their offspring is, however, now attracting considerable attention.

It is widely believed that most couples in Western countries would prefer to have a son first, followed by a daughter. However, a recent survey conducted in the UK by Gallup (see diagram for details) suggests that this view is something of an oversimplification. Certainly more people professed a preference for a boy rather than a girl for their first child and for a girl rather than a boy for the second, but even more said that they had no preference. In response to a further question, 82% of the total said that they would not like to choose the sex of their children.

In poor countries there are sometimes strong economic arguments in favor of having sons rather than daughters. Sons can support their parents in old age, whereas the need to provide a dowry for a daughter at the time of her marriage can prove a heavy parental liability.

Few people would question the desirability of being able to preselect a child's sex in cases where families have a history of hereditary diseases such as hemophilia and some types of muscular dystrophy. Symptoms of these diseases are displayed only by men, but they are inherited through the mother. Such couples are often reluctant to risk having children; if they knew they would have only daughters, the problem would be solved.

At present, the only sure way of ensuring that a child will be of the desired sex is to ascertain the sex of the fetus by amniocentesis — analysis of the amniotic fluid — and then to abort any fetus of the wrong sex. Obviously, the possibility of preselecting gender at conception is a much more attractive proposition.

Several researchers into sex determination now claim high success rates for preselection techniques. Based on claimed differences in the physiology and behavior of X and Y sperm, these techniques involve such factors as the timing, frequency and manner of intercourse, the eating of certain foods before intercourse, and the use of artificial insemination. A selection of methods is described in more detail on subsequent pages. Other scientists, however, remain highly skeptical, whereas some sociologists are worried about the implications of sex preselection on the balance of the sexes.

### The stronger sex?
Although male (Y) and female (X) sperm are produced in equal numbers, research by Dr Landrum B. Shettles shows big differences in performance. At conception (A), there are 160 males for every 100 females. But male zygotes prove less hardy, and by implantation (B) the ratio is 120 to 100. At birth (C) males outnumber females by 105 to 100.

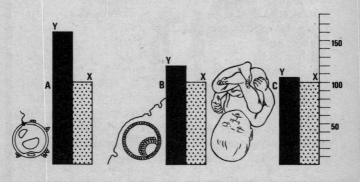

© DIAGRAM

# Preselecting gender 2

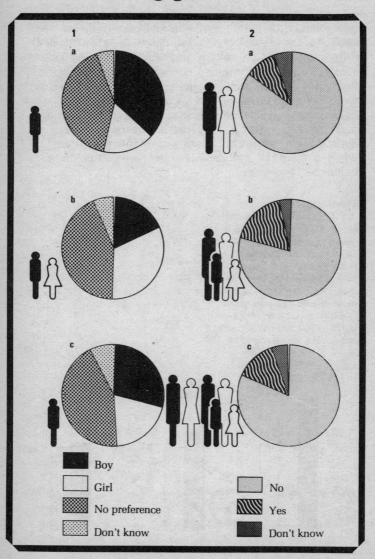

Boy
Girl
No preference
Don't know

No
Yes
Don't know

# Physiology of sex

**If they could choose** (*left*)

These diagrams are based on details of a survey conducted in the UK in March 1980 by Gallup (and included here by courtesy of the BBC).

**1** Asked how they would choose if they were able to choose the sex of a child:

**a** for a first child, 37% would choose a boy, 16% a girl, 41% had no preference, 5% didn't know;

**b** for a second child, 18% would choose a boy, 32% a girl, 43% had no preference, 6% didn't know;

**c** for an only child, 29% would choose a boy, 20% a girl, 44% had no preference, 7% didn't know.

**2** Asked whether they would like to choose the sex of a child if this were possible:

**a** of people with no children, 85% said no, 10% yes, and 5% didn't know;

**b** of people with children, 78% said no, 19% yes, and 3% didn't know;

**c** of all people asked, 82% said no, 13% yes, and 4% didn't know.

**Balance of the sexes** (*below*)

Our diagram (based on United Nations figures for 1975) shows how many extra males or females there are for every 100 members of the opposite sex.

**a** World 0.4 males
**b** Asia 3.9 males
**c** Oceania 2.9 males
**d** C. and S. America 0.2 males
**e** Africa 1.2 females
**f** N. America 4.5 females
**g** Europe 5.2 females
**h** USSR 15.3 females

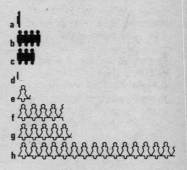

© DIAGRAM

43

# Preselection methods 1

**Male and female sperm**
The only uncontested difference between "male" and "female" sperm is in the shape of the chromosome that bears the sex factor. High-magnification (**a**) shows that this chromosome is X-shaped for females and Y-shaped for males. Some scientists, however, now claim that male and female sperm are differentiated in other ways. Our drawing (**b**) illustrates the claim made by Dr Landrum B. Shettles that male sperm have a smaller head and longer tail than female sperm. Shettles and other researchers into sex preselection go on to argue that physiological and also behavioral differences between male and female sperm can be exploited by couples wishing to choose the sex of their offspring.

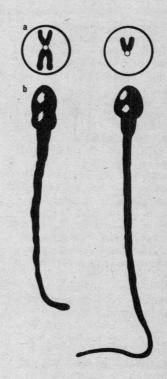

**Artificial insemination**
More boys than girls result from artificial insemination. This may stem from the fact that male (Y) sperm is lighter than female (X) sperm. When semen is stored in a container, Y sperm collect at the top and X sperm at the bottom. Samples from different levels show the top third to be 80% Y, the bottom third 80% X and the middle third about 50% of each.

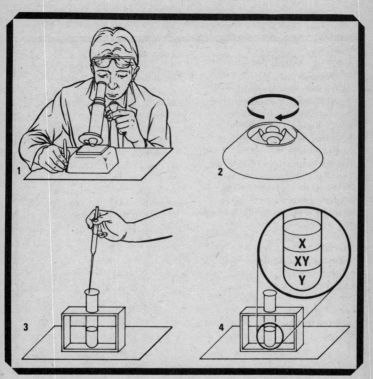

## Sperm separation

Unconfirmed experiments by Dr R. Ericson and some US fertility clinics suggest that the following method can be used to influence the sex of children conceived through artificial insemination.

**1** A microscope is used to check normality of sperm in semen.

**2** Semen is spun in a centrifuge to separate healthiest sperm.

**3** These sperm are transferred to a test tube containing albumen.

**4** Research suggests that many more male sperm swim down through the albumen, to give a claimed 85% concentration of male sperm at the bottom of the tube after a 4 hour interval.

©DIAGRAM

# Preselection methods 2

## For a boy
1  Couple abstain from intercourse until just after the calculated time of ovulation.
2  With medical approval, the woman before intercourse applies an alkaline douche of 2 tablespoons of baking soda in 1 quart of water.
3  Man penetrates as deeply as possible during intercourse.
4  Woman experiences orgasm, releasing a secretion in the cervix that helps neutralize the acid in the vagina.

## For a girl
1  Couple continue intercourse until 2 days before ovulation and then abstain.
2  With medical approval, the woman before intercourse applies an acid douche of 2 tablespoons of vinegar in 1 quart of water.
3  Penetration during intercourse should be shallow.
4  Woman does not have an orgasm, so helping preserve acidity in the vagina.

## Shettles' method
Dr Landrum B. Shettles and his followers claim that sperm carrying the male factor are less hardy but can swim faster than sperm carrying the female factor. Shettles' sex preselection method — with a claimed success rate of 80-85% — recommends couples to take advantage of these differences by following various procedures intended to create conditions that are more favorable to sperm with the required sex factor.

**For a boy**
Salt, salty cheese, sausages, ham, tea, coffee

**For a girl**
Eggs, milk

## Food chooses the sex

Studies suggest that once in a woman's genital tract, X sperm like surroundings rich in calcium and magnesium, whereas Y sperm prefer potassium. Some researchers believe that eating foods containing these different elements will favor one type of sperm over the other. Examples of recommended foods are listed above the illustrations. In one Canadian test group, 81% of the women are claimed to have had a baby of the sex they wanted.

©DIAGRAM

# Sex differentiation 1

In the first few weeks, male and female embryos look alike.
Even male and female sex organs begin identically. Male sex
organs start differing from female sex organs when XY
chromosomes in the male embryo instruct gonads (sex
glands) to produce the male hormone testosterone. This
starts all-male structures growing, while another
(Müllerian-inhibiting) hormone suppresses female
structures that were already being formed.

External genital organs develop from a swelling in the wall
of a cavity within the body of the embryo. In the male this
swelling turns into a penis. In the female it becomes a
clitoris. In males, two folds of the swelling join so that the
urethra exits through the penis; in the female, the folds form
the inner vaginal lips. A swelling around the genital
opening turns into the scrotum (in males) or into the
female's outer vaginal lips and mount of Venus (the raised
area of fatty tissue in front of the pubic bone).

Meanwhile internal genital organs take shape. From the
genital ridge projecting into the embryo's body cavity come
gonads that eventually differentiate into the male testes or
female ovaries (first distinguished by the testes' fibrous
covering). Also two important pairs of tubes evolve. The
Müllerian tubes (or ducts) produce the female's Fallopian
tubes, and fuse to make her uterus and vagina. In males, the
Müllerian tubes degenerate surviving only as a cul-de-sac
inside the prostate gland. In males the Wolffian tubes
develop into the tubes leading from the testes. In females it
is the Wolffian tubes that degenerate and tend to disappear.

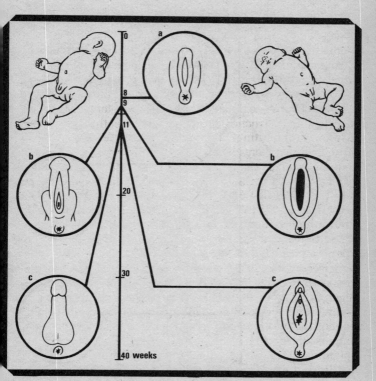

## Development of sexual organs
Time scales numbered in weeks
from the expectant mother's last
menstruation are here used to
show stages in the divergence of
external and internal sex organs
in male and female embryos.

## External organs
**a** At 8 weeks male and female
are still both alike.
**b** At 9 weeks the male's penis
grows longer, and in females the
disappearance of a membrane
opens up the primitive vagina.
**c** At 11 weeks the male's
urogenital groove has closed, and
in females the external genitals
take shape.

© DIAGRAM

# Sex differentiation 2

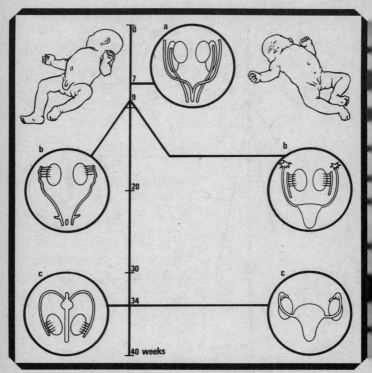

## Internal organs

**a** At 7 weeks male and female are still both alike.

**b** At 9 weeks the Müllerian tubes are lost in males, and the Wolffian tubes are almost lost in females.

**c** At 34 weeks the male's gonads migrate to the scrotum, becoming testes linked to the urethra by the vas deferens. In females the gonads become ovaries; the nearby Fallopian tubes, derived from the Müllerian tubes, will during the reproductive years convey ripe eggs from the ovaries to the uterus.

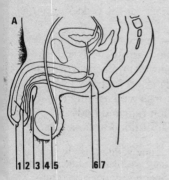

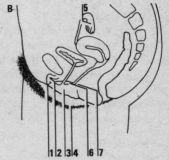

## Sexual parallels

Although the sexual systems of an adult man (**A**) and woman (**B**) differ, they show parallels of form and function consequent upon their development from the same simple embryonic structures.

**1** The head of the penis and of the clitoris consist of sensory tissue.

**2** The shaft of the penis and of the clitoris have erectile tissue.

**3** Soft tissue makes up the underside of the penis and the inner vaginal lips.

**4** Hair grows on the scrotum and on the outer vaginal lips.

**5** Testes and ovaries both make reproductive cells.

**6** The bulb of the penis and the woman's vestibular bulbs comprise erectile tissue.

**7** Cowper's gland in a man and Bartholin's glands in a woman make lubricating fluids.

# Development at puberty 1

The "watershed" of puberty is reached when girls start ovulating and boys producing sperm. Meanwhile, physical, emotional and psychological changes affect the entire body. In most of these, boys will lag a year or more behind girls. But by the late teens, males and females both have mature sexual organs and well-developed secondary sexual characteristics. Before the onset of puberty, girls and boys share a similar body shape. But by their late teens boys have become taller and more muscular than girls, with broader shoulders, and also facial hair. Girls gain a rounded form produced by widened hips and enlarged breasts, which equip them for the tasks of giving birth and suckling babies.

Both sexes share certain changes to the body. Skin grows oilier and coarser, and sweat glands grow more active. Gland secretions produce blackheads and acne. Armpits and genitals begin emitting body odor. As body tissues grow, blood volume and pressure as well as lung capacity increase; but heart rate, respiration rate and body temperature all tend to drop as adulthood approaches.

### How boys develop

Illustrations of a boy at ages 10, 12, 14 and 18 show a typical developmental pattern. There are, however, considerable individual variations.

By the age of 10 a boy has reached 78% of adult height, but only 45% of adult weight. His testes are only 10% of their adult size. Facial and underarm hair have not yet appeared.

Some boys grow fat when aged about 11, before puberty arrives. By 12 the testes and scrotum are growing larger. The penis also grows and now erects spontaneously more often than

formerly. Pubic hair appears and later assumes its adult coloration. Sperm secretion starts and ejaculation may occur in sleep, though sperm may be too immature to fertilize an ovum. The prostate gland has become enlarged by now, and changes in the larynx deepen the voice.

By 14 the boy has reached 91% of adult height and 70% of adult weight. The shoulders have grown broader, and muscular strength has rapidly increased. By 18 the body has reached 99% of adult size and 92% of adult weight.

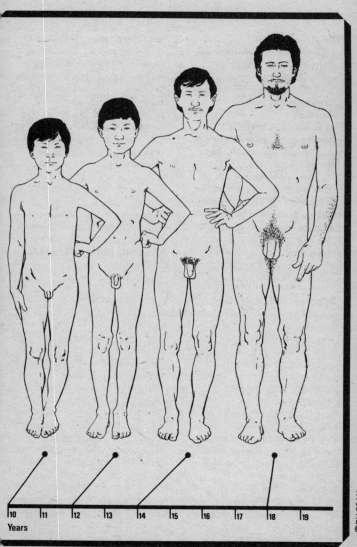

# Development at puberty 2

**How girls develop**

A typical female developmental pattern is here shown by illustrations of a girl aged 10, 11, 14 and 16. As with boys there are considerable individual variations.

By the age of 10, a girl has reached 83% of adult height but only 53% of adult weight. Her body form is like a boy's. The body's so-called adolescent growth spurt usually starts about age 10. Most girls have not yet developed breasts or pubic or underarm hair. The uterus is about half adult size and the ovaries about one-third adult size. These and other sex organs now begin to grow rapidly.

By 11 the nipples become more prominent and the breasts start to develop. The pelvis widens and fatty pads appear on the hips. Hair starts growing under arms and in the pubic area; later it grows coarser, darker and curlier. The girl may reach the menarche (start menstruating) at 13. Ovulation begins slightly later, perhaps at age 14. By now the girl has reached 97% of her adult height and 85% of her adult weight.

From 14 to 16 the breasts continue to grow, skeletal growth stops, the genitals mature, and the menstrual periods become fully regular.

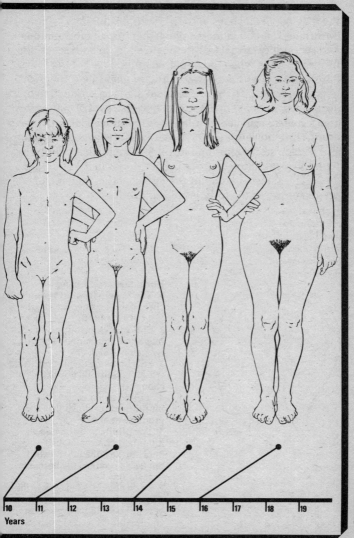

Years

# Hormones at puberty 1

Puberty occurs as boys and girls start producing certain hormones (chemical messengers) that instruct the genitals and secondary sexual features to develop. In both sexes, the process begins when the hypothalamus, a part of the lower brain, stimulates the nearby pituitary gland by a chemical releasing factor. The pituitary then starts to produce two hormones involved in the sexual development of both males and females: follicle-stimulating hormone (FSH) and luteinizing hormone (LH). These hormones act on the male and female sex organs, and development further continues with the production of other sex hormones in the sex organs themselves: testosterone in the testes, and estrogen and progesterone in the follicles of the ovaries.

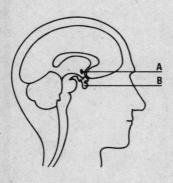

**Hormonal action in males**
1 The hypothalamus (**A**) sends a chemical releasing factor to the pituitary gland (**B**).
2 This causes the pituitary to release follicle-stimulating hormone (FSH).
3 FSH helps sperm manufacture, which is controlled by the chemical inhibin.
4 Inhibin is fed back to the pituitary to cut down the production of FSH.
5 The pituitary also releases luteinizing hormone (LH).
6 LH makes interstitial cells in the testes produce the hormone testosterone.
7 Testosterone is fed back to the pituitary, and helps the development of male genitals and secondary sexual features.

**Key**

- Releasing factor
- Inhibin
- Follicle-stimulating hormone (FSH)
- Luteinizing hormone (LH)
- Testosterone

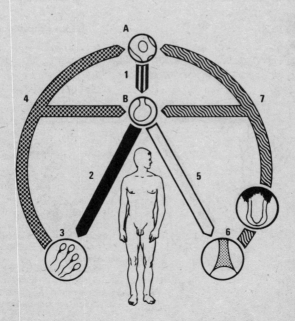

# Hormones at puberty 2

**Hormonal action in females**

**1** The hypothalamus (**A**) directs a releasing factor to the pituitary (**B**).
**2** The pituitary releases FSH.
**3** FSH stimulates the growth of egg follicles in the ovaries.
**4** The egg follicles then start producing estrogen.
**5** Estrogen helps the genitals and breasts to develop.
**6** The build-up of estrogen in the bloodstream causes the hypothalamus and pituitary to cut down FSH production.

**7** It also causes the pituitary to start releasing LH.
**8** LH makes one follicle burst to free its egg for fertilization.
**9** The corpus luteum (empty follicle) produces progesterone.
**10** Progesterone makes the uterus lining ready to receive and feed a fertilized egg.
**11** If no egg is fertilized, estrogen and progesterone levels in the bloodstream fall after approximately 14 days and menstruation occurs.

▬▬▬ Releasing factor

▬▬▬ FSH

☐ LH

▨ Estrogen

▨ Progesterone

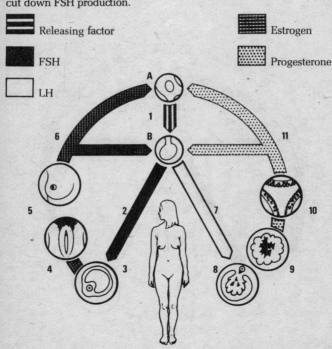

## The menstrual cycle

The start of menstruation is the most obvious indication of the onset of puberty in a female. This diagram shows the role of different hormones during the monthly cycle. Changing levels of FSH (**a**), estrogen (**b**), LH (**c**), and progesterone (**d**) produce the cycle's features: the maturing and releasing of an egg (**e**), changes in the quantity and character of cervical mucus (**f**) which is abundant, thin and clear at the time of ovulation, and the building up of the uterus lining or endometrium (**g**) to receive a fertilized egg, and its breaking down and shedding at menstruation (**h**) which occurs if no egg is fertilized. (Also see pp. 160-161.)

# Male sex organs 1

Man's primary sex glands are the testes: two egg-shaped organs hanging in the scrotum, a visible sac behind and below the penis. Testes produce sperm cells and the male hormones called androgens. Sperm is stored in the epididymides for transfer via two tubes (vas deferens) to the urethra. On the way, sperm cells mix with seminal fluid from the seminal vesicles, prostate gland and Cowper's gland. The resulting mixture is the thick white liquid called semen. Like urine from the bladder, semen travels through the urethra to exit from the penis tip.

**Male genital system**
Major parts of the male genital system are here shown together with the area around them, mainly those parts involved in the elimination of body waste products.
**a** Bladder
**b** Vas deferens
**c** Seminal vesicles
**d** Pubic bone
**e** Prostate gland
**f** Rectum
**g** Cowper's gland
**h** Urethra
**i** Penis
**j** Anus
**k** Epididymis
**l** Testis
**m** Scrotum

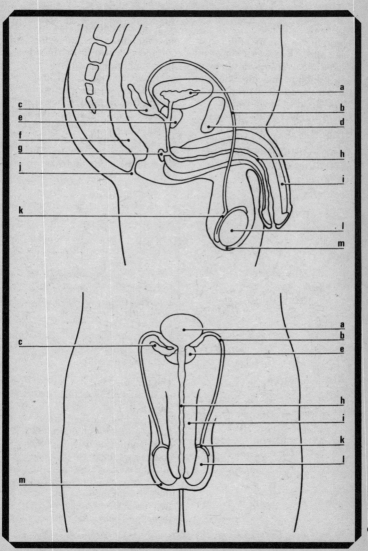

# Male sex organs 2

## The penis

The cylindrical shape of the penis allows it to enter a woman's vagina and so ensure the internal fertilization of an ovum. The penis of most adult males is about 3¼-4¼in long, and normally hangs limply. For intercourse it becomes stiff, enlarged, erect and usually 5-7in long. Shown here are a longitudinal section (**1**) and a cross section (**2**).

Skin (**a**) and fibrous tissue (**b**) surround three spongy erectile cylinders. Two (**c**) lie side by side above the third (**d**) which encloses the urethra (**e**). This ends in a slit-shaped opening, the meatus (**f**). The head of the lower cylinder is the glans penis (**g**), a cone that fits over the ends of the two upper cylinders. Loose skin covers all but the penis tip. The foreskin (**h**), a skin fold that

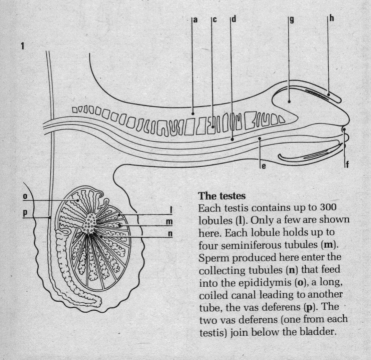

## The testes

Each testis contains up to 300 lobules (**l**). Only a few are shown here. Each lobule holds up to four seminiferous tubules (**m**). Sperm produced here enter the collecting tubules (**n**) that feed into the epididymis (**o**), a long, coiled canal leading to another tube, the vas deferens (**p**). The two vas deferens (one from each testis) join below the bladder.

## Physiology of sex

conceals the glans penis, is cut off in circumcision, an operation sometimes performed for social, religious or medical reasons. The penis is supplied with nerves (**i**), and variations of bloodflow — in via arteries (**j**) and out via veins (**k**) — determine whether a penis is limp or erect. (See also p. 105.)

### Sperm production

Sperm are produced at 3-4°F below body temperature, which is why the testes hang free below the body. In a seminiferous tubule, spermatogonia cells (**1**) near the tubule wall split in two to produce spermatocytes (**2**) that give rise to spermatids (**3**). These evolve into spermatozoons (**4**) — sperm cells that mature in the epididymis and vas deferens.

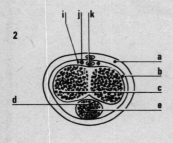

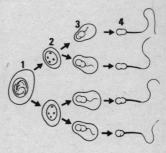

### Sperm

A sperm is here shown much enlarged. Chromosomes in the head (**A**) pass on hereditary material during fertilization. The body (**B**) gives energy to a tail (**C**) that lashes the sperm through seminal fluid at 3-7in per hour. Sperm are microscopically tiny and one man produces over 500 million a day. Sperm not ejaculated soon decay and are absorbed by the body.

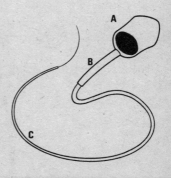

©DIAGRAM

# Female sex organs 1

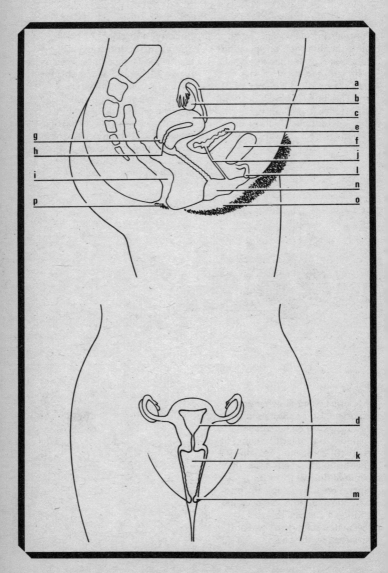

# Physiology of sex

A woman's internal sex organs are units that work in three main ways. First, there are two production units that store and ripen eggs. Second, there is a safe, well-nourished chamber where a fertilized egg can lodge and grow into a baby. Third, there are three tubes connected with that chamber. These tubes help a sperm to reach and fertilize an egg inside the woman's body, and one of them later lets out the baby resulting from this union of male and female cells. Ovaries are the two organs producing eggs, and the female hormones estrogen and progesterone. Each month an egg leaves an ovary and is collected by a Fallopian tube, in

**Internal female genitals**
These diagrams show side and front views of major parts of the female internal genital system, and nearby areas.

**a** Fallopian tube
**b** Ovary
**c** Uterus (womb)
**d** Endometrium
**e** Bladder
**f** Pubic bone
**g** Cervix
**h** Os
**i** Rectum
**j** Urethra
**k** Vagina
**l** Clitoris
**m** Bartholin's glands
**n** Labia minora
**o** Labia majora
**p** Anus

# Female sex organs 2

which eggs are usually fertilized. To reach this tube, sperm are ejected from a partner's penis inserted into the vagina. This muscular passage is up to 5 inches long, and narrow, though it can be stretched to take a penis, and much more in childbirth. Fluid secreted by vagina and cervix clean the vagina. The inner end of the vagina leads to the os, a narrow opening in the cervix, the lower end of the uterus. This organ, normally about the size and shape of a pear, is walled with muscle and lined with the endometrium. This mucous membrane nourishes a fertilized egg after it has moved down its Fallopian tube into the uterus and become implanted in the wall. The menstrual cycle in non-pregnant women involves monthly changes to the endometrium (see pages 160-161).

Inside the uterus, the fertilized egg develops into an embryo, then a fetus, whose growth stretches the uterus like a balloon. Muscular contractions force the full-term baby from the uterus out through the vagina.

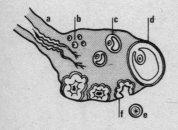

**Egg production**
At birth each ovary (**a**) holds a lifetime's supply of one million microscopic unripe eggs in sacs called follicles (**b**). Only 125,000 reach puberty. Throughout a woman's sexual life only about 200 eggs per ovary mature (**c,d**) and leave the ovary (**e**). Emptied follicles (**f**) and "failed" eggs remain inside the ovary, where they regress and are absorbed.

# Physiology of sex

## External female genitals

Called collectively the vulva, and largely hidden by pubic hair, these lie between the legs. The vaginal opening (**a**) is partly covered by a membrane called the hymen (**b**) and lies below the urinary outlet or urethra (**c**) and above the anus (**d**). Mucus from Bartholin's glands (**e**) lubricates the inner lips, or labia minora (**f**), hairless skin folds that flank the vagina. Above the urethra they fuse to form a clitoral hood (**g**) masking the clitoris (**h**), a female "penis." The fatty outer lips or labia majora (**i**) extend down from the mons veneris (mons pubis) — a fatty pad over the pubic bone — to form the vulva's protective rim. The perineum (**j**) is a skin triangle that covers tissue stretched in childbirth.

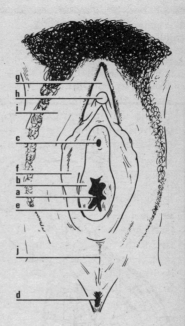

## The hymen

Also called the maidenhead, this thin fold of tissue partly shuts the vaginal opening (**1**). It may be ring shaped (**2**) or perforated. Sometimes it completely seals the vagina and must be cut in a minor operation before menstruation begins. Petting or inserting tampons stretches the hymen and first intercourse may rupture it, causing some pain and bleeding.

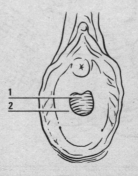

# Chapter 3

1  A whimsical depiction of childhood sexuality.
2  An adolescent girl admires her developing breasts in this 19th century illustration by German cartoonist Heinrich Ziller.

2

# Childhood sexuality 1

The foundations of adult sexuality are largely built during early childhood. Until the work of Sigmund Freud it was thought that children had no sexual feelings until puberty. Now it is generally accepted that very young children have sexual feelings and are intensely curious about sex. Sex becomes woven into their fantasies. As early as their second year they may begin what Freud called sexual researches— observing adults, listening for scraps of information and tying together various infantile theories, principally to explain where babies come from.

Children quickly become interested in the intimacy they observe between their parents. They want to know what happens in the parental bedroom. However, direct observation of parental sex, what Freud called the primal scene, upsets children. They lack sufficient real information to explain what they see and often conclude that sex is a form of violent struggle. Often it is not possible to protect children from primal scene experience of some sort. Attitudes to sex are affected by the home environment. Parental disapproval is absorbed into the personality and becomes an internal watchdog, a type of conscience.

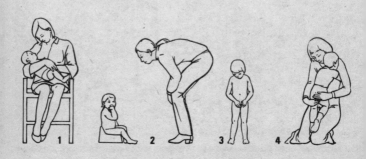

# Discovering sexuality

**Stages of sexual development**
According to Freud, childhood
sexuality develops in stages.
**1  The oral stage** persists through
the first year; pleasure, from
sucking and eating, is centered
on the mouth.
**2  The anal stage** begins around
age 2. Potty training becomes an
important challenge. Now
feelings of excitement are located
in the anus. The child derives
pleasure from retaining and
expelling feces.
**3  The phallic stage** begins
around the start of the third year.
Interest centers on the penis,
which is overvalued. Boys fear
castration as a sexual
punishment. Girls are said to
envy penises and worry that they
are castrated males.
**4  The Oedipus complex**
develops at age 2 or 3, when
attachment to the parent of the
opposite sex becomes deeply
possessive and passionate. The
child fantasizes about killing the
other parent.
**5  Latency** sets in after year 5,
when sexual interest becomes
repressed until puberty.
**6  The genital stage** is mature
adult sexuality, whose healthy
aim is intercourse with a life
partner.

5

6

© DIAGRAM

# Childhood sexuality 2

**Stages of sexual interest**
A child's interest in sex is likely to vary according to the following approximate time scale.

**A 0-18 months** At some time in the first year a child discovers its own sex organs and handles them in much the same way that it handles its fingers and toes.

**B 18 months-3 years** A child now finds that the sex organs bring pleasure, and may start to masturbate. Awareness of genital differences between the sexes may also begin.

**C 3-5 years** A child is now more aware of the differences between male and female sex organs, and may be worried by this. There may be some sex play between boys and girls of this age, and most children now develop a curiosity about the "facts of life."

**D 5-7 years** Sex play or mild exhibitionism is likely to continue until around age 7. Although overt sexual curiosity may die down slightly, interest

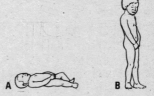

in sex tends to continue in a different, more clandestine form.

**E 8-11 years** From about the age of 8 or 9 most children develop an interest in swearing, "smutty" jokes, and pictures of sex. Sex, too, becomes a major topic of discussion with friends.

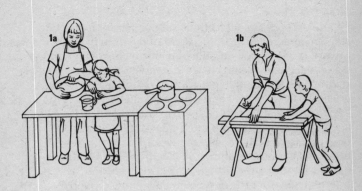

## Gender roles

Gender role behavior is to a great extent established during childhood. Boys and girls tend to follow the behavior patterns demonstrated by their parents and to learn from them such things as how to relate to members of the opposite sex and what types of work and displays of emotion are appropriate to members of each sex. In most Western countries, girls have traditionally been taught to be homeloving, passive and subservient, whereas boys have been encouraged to be outgoing, self-reliant and not to show their emotions. Recent years have seen a blurring of traditional gender stereotypes as more and more activities are accepted as equally appropriate to males or females. Our illustrations show children learning activities from a parent of the same sex (1a,1b) and of the opposite sex (2a,2b).

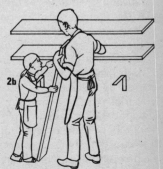

©DIAGRAM

# Adolescent sexuality 1

At adolescence sexual feelings submerged in the latency
stage reemerge powerfully as part of the growth spurt
toward physical and emotional maturity. Sexual longings,
self-consciousness and an acute awareness of the opposite
sex replace the relative placidity of childhood. Identity
crises and great social and emotional challenges follow.
Masturbation at this time is both a comfort and an outlet for
acute sexual tension. But old myths and hypocrisy about
masturbation die hard, and many adolescents suffer
unnecessary anxiety and guilt. Nearly all boys fantasize
during masturbation, usually imagining sex play or
intercourse with girls or women they know or whose
pictures they have seen. Fewer girls fantasize when they
masturbate. Fantasies of young adolescent girls are usually
less specifically erotic than those of boys or older girls, and
include more thoughts of romance and emotional
attachment. Adolescents of both sexes develop "crushes"
on teachers, movie actors or pop stars.

With the onset of adolescence the teenager is flooded with
sexual feelings that are difficult to channel. Fleeting
homosexual encounters are an easy way to gain some sexual
experience. These also gratify a natural curiosity about the
sex organs. Both boys and girls are often eager to gain access
to sexual literature, and this, too, stems from a mixture of
curiosity and a desire to be stimulated.

Adolescence is also a time of doubt. Boys may imagine that
their penises are too small or too large. They may be anxious
about homosexuality or worry that they are girlish in
manner or appearance. Girls are often embarrassed about
their breasts, imagining they are not standard in size for
their age. Some girls delay the challenges and anxieties of
adult sexuality by putting on or losing excessive amounts of
weight or by dressing in a drab or unfashionable manner.
The help that parents could offer is often unavailable
because of shyness on both sides. An American study
showed that parents felt with relief that once a sexual topic

had been discussed it was "over and done with." Mothers were approached for sexual information much more often than fathers.

Dating is an important feature of the adolescent years and frequent changes of partner typically precede the choice of a marriage partner. The eventual break with the parental home is often difficult and feelings of sadness are hidden beneath the angry clashes characteristic of parent-child relations at this time.

**Influences**
Adolescence is the time when an individual starts to develop his or her own sexual code and values. At first the strongest influence comes from the parents (**1**), but as adolescence proceeds ideas derived from the parents are typically superseded by views influenced more by school, the media and, most important, the adolescent's peer group (**2**).

©DIAGRAM

# Adolescent sexuality 2

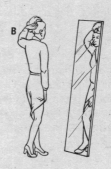

**Gender roles** (*above*)
The imposition of traditional
gender roles has been a cause of
much misery and confusion to
adolescents. Boys have been
encouraged to define
adolescence in terms of sexual
success (**A**), whereas girls have
been faced with reconciling
society's demands that they be
both sexually attractive and
sexually restrained (**B**).

**Guilt at masturbation** (*below*)
Although masturbation is very
common among adolescents,
many of them worry about it. In
his book *Adolescent Sexuality
in Contemporary America*
(1973), Robert C. Sorensen gives
the following data on how often
masturbation caused feelings of
guilt, anxiety or concern among
his sample of adolescents with
current masturbatory experience.

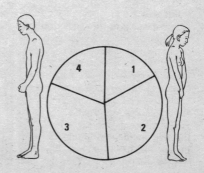

1  Often 17%.
2  Sometimes 32%.
3  Rarely 32%.
4  Never 19%.

## Sex and love

Although adolescents show an obvious and sometimes obsessive interest in sex, the majority believe that sex is not the most important aspect of a loving relationship. R.C. Sorensen's study group of US adolescents replied as follows when asked whether they agreed that "the most important thing in a loving relationship is sex."

**A** Boys aged 13-15:
69% disagreed, 31% agreed.
**B** Girls aged 13-15:
77% disagreed, 3% were not sure, 20% agreed.
**C** Boys aged 16-19:
84% disagreed, 16% agreed.
**D** Girls aged 16-19:
94% disagreed, 2% were not sure, 4% agreed.

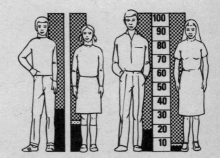

Disagreed
Were not sure
Agreed

©DIAGRAM

# Adult sexuality 1

By the late teens physical maturity has been attained, but it is a misconception that adult psychosexual maturity automatically follows. Although adolescence is a time of experimentation there is a tendency to exaggerate the extent of teenage sexual experience. Sometimes isolation from the opposite sex, caused by shyness or by practical factors, such as years in single-sex boarding schools, results in sexually naive adults.

Experience of sexual intercourse usually begins in early adulthood, often before marriage. This is an important time. Young women may be scared of penetration, fearing pain or a sense of humiliation. Men are afraid of their inexperience, that they will perform badly. Some have lingering guilt feelings. These problems may result in impotence or premature ejaculation in men and in vaginal pain or lack of orgasm in women. First experiences can greatly help or hinder confidence. A caring, tolerant partner is crucial, particularly for women, who often fear they will be abandoned after the man is satisfied. Some women only become orgasmic in their thirties or forties. Many men learn orgasm control by delaying orgasm in masturbation, a method prescribed by sex therapists.

Sexual maturity does not begin and end with the

achievement of orgasm control in men and orgasmic capacity in women. In the first years of marriage sexual activity is often high and pleasure intense. One later danger is that married sex may become a routine that is boring to both partners. Now the challenge is to keep sex alive in marriage. Partners may discover in themselves desires for different types of sexual experience with their mates. Men may, for example, wish to indulge in mild fetishism by having their wives dress in certain types of clothing. Women may wish for play-acted violence in sex. These wishes are not "perverse." They are not part of immature sexuality. They are part of a person's sexual nature which may emerge more clearly as a relationship progresses beyond the early phases.

According to Freud sexual maturity is reached when the fantasies and activities that excited us as children are gathered into what he called "genital maturity." This stage is reached when the final aim of the sexual instinct is genital intercourse with a life partner. What he called infantile sexuality may be present in a mild form in sexual foreplay. One of the main pitfalls in marriage or any close sexual relationship is dependency. Even at a mature physical age people carry within them some of the needs of early

# Adult sexuality 2

childhood, particularly the wish to be looked after by a loving parent-figure. Powerful dependency needs can seriously disrupt a relationship. Some people cope with fears of dependency by nymphomania, in which a woman turns rapidly from partner to partner, or by compulsive male promiscuity. In both of these the hectic search for partners expresses a demand for more and more love. Thanks to the quick change of partners, however, independence is preserved. People demonstrating this pattern of activity never become totally dependent on one partner.

Although the sex drive declines with age, the rate and extent

**Stages in adult sexuality**
Sexual activity among Western adults commonly corresponds to a four-stage pattern.
**1 Young adult/mate selection**
Levels of sexual activity and romantic commitment increase. Premarital intercourse is common. Embarrassment and secrecy about sexual activity disappear. Family, friends and media apply pressure to marry.

**2 Young adult/early marriage**
Sexual activity is legitimized by marriage. The level of sexual activity is high. Many couples experiment with different sexual techniques. Birth of children may be followed by a decline in eroticism.

of this decline are often exaggerated. In fact, desire and capacity for intercourse are often retained into extreme old age. Sometimes, however, fears of social disapproval and worries about unattractiveness or sexual performance may lead a couple to give up sexual activity prematurely. Greater understanding of the sexual problems of old people is badly needed, particularly in view of increased longevity.

The physically and mentally handicapped are other groups whose sexual problems need special understanding. In many areas the last few years have seen an encouraging trend toward greater availability of specialist help.

**3 Middle years of marriage**
Marital intercourse rates fall. Dissatisfaction may lead to extramarital affairs. Work commitments may cause marital problems. Nonsexual aspects of marriage become increasingly important to marital stability and continuity.

**4 Later years of marriage**
Sexual activity declines still further as physical energy and attractiveness decrease. Children have left home. Other nonsexual commitments provide marriage with its basis.

©DIAGRAM

# Chapter 4

# Attraction and courtship

A lover symbolically offers his heart in this romantic cut-out silhouette.

# Physical attraction 1

People are attracted to each other usually because they admire qualities or characteristics in the other person. Such admiration is often initially founded on physical appearance for this is the first thing we notice about a new acquaintance. When we meet someone new, we take note of their appearance — often subconsciously — and react accordingly: if they are physically attractive we may try to hold their attention and attempt to get to know them better, but if they are unattractive a relationship is less likely to develop.

Surveys have found that people who are believed to be

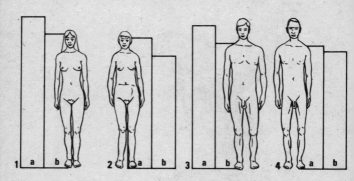

**Attitudes and attractiveness**
For this study (D. Byrne, 1970), US students were paired for a "blind date" with a partner whose attitudes were either similar or dissimilar to their own. When later asked to rate their partners, the students showed a preference for physical attractiveness rather than similarity of views.

1 **Attractive female:**
a similar attitudes 12.7;
b dissimilar attitudes 11.3.
2 **Unattractive female:**
a similar attitudes 11.0;
b dissimilar attitudes 9.5.
3 **Attractive male:**
a similar attitudes 12.0;
b dissimilar attitudes 10.6.
4 **Unattractive male:**
a similar attitudes 10.4;
b dissimilar attitudes 9.9.

physically attractive are also thought to be more successful, confident and popular, and also happier than those who are thought to be unattractive. Physical attraction, it seems, gives people a head start not only in the mating game but also in life in general. Luckily for most of us, however, ideas of beauty vary greatly from person to person, from culture to culture, and even from year to year. Ideas of physical attractiveness are considerably influenced by advertising, television and movies, but even here, when it comes to making personal choices, almost everyone is prepared to settle for something rather less than the plastic ideal.

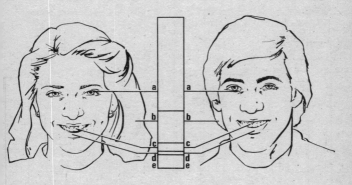

**Face to face**
A survey conducted in the UK by National Opinion Polls in 1976 indicated that the eyes, chosen by 62% of those asked, are the most attractive feature of the face and head. Hair came a poor second with 22% of the vote.
**a** Eyes 62%.
**b** Hair 22%.
**c** Teeth 5%.
**d** Mouth 3%.
**e** Other 8%.

©DIAGRAM

# Physical attraction 2

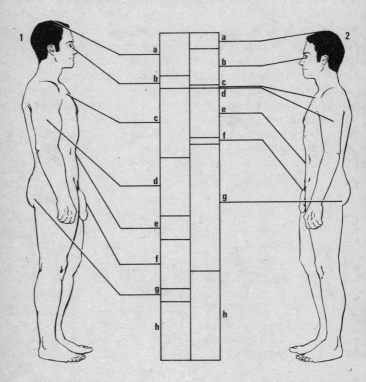

**The macho myth**

A survey conducted in the USA by *Village Voice* asked men what they thought women found most attractive about the male body and then asked women what they actually did admire most.

**1 What men believe women admire**

a  Tallness 13%.
b  Eyes 4%.
c  Muscular chest/shoulders 21%.
d  Muscular arms 18%.

e  Slimness 7%.
f  Large penis 15%.
g  Buttocks 4%.
h  Other 18%.

**2 What women actually admire**

a  Tallness 5%.
b  Eyes 11%.
c  Muscular chest/shoulders 1%.
d  Muscular arms 0%.
e  Slimness 15%.
f  Penis 2%.
g  Buttocks 39%.
h  Other 27%.

# Attraction and courtship

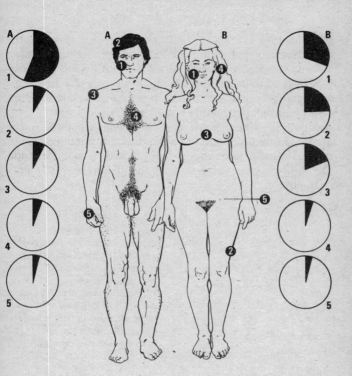

## The body beautiful

A recent survey conducted in the UK asked men and women which part of the body they found most attractive in members of the opposite sex. Here we indicate the five body parts of men (**A**) and women (**B**) that received the highest percentages of votes. Both men and women seem to be especially attracted by faces, but the percentage of women who voted the face first in the survey was higher than the comparable vote among men.

**Top five male attributes**
1 Face 55%.
2 Hair 8%.
3 Shoulders 7%.
4 Chest 6%.
5 Hands 4%.

**Top five female attributes**
1 Face 32%.
2 Legs 24%.
3 Bust 18%.
4 Hair 5%.
5 Bottom 4%.

©DIAGRAM

# Other attraction factors 1

Here we look at some of the factors other than physical attractiveness that are influential in the attraction process. As we get to know a person better, personality and practical factors tend to become more important than physical attractiveness in determining whether or not a relationship will continue. Personality factors affecting mutual compatibility include whether or not one or both partners are by nature dominant or submissive, confident or timid, serious-minded or happy-go-lucky. Practical factors include the ability of one partner to meet the material requirements of the other.

**Like or unlike self**
Some people find that they are usually attracted to people who are very like themselves — in terms of temperament, interests and sometimes even in their physical appearance (**A**). Other people find that they are much more attracted to people with very different characteristics that complement their own (**B**).

# Attraction and courtship

## Like father, like mother

Similarity to the parent of the opposite sex is thought by some psychologists to be an important factor when it comes to choosing a mate. Women are said to be attracted to men who resemble their fathers (**C**), while men are thought to look for women who remind them of their mothers (**D**).

## Choosing a life style

As well as being attracted by a potential partner's appearance and personality, many people are influenced by the type of life style that they might expect with that partner. Perhaps the ideal is a simple home life with lots of children (**E**), or maybe the attraction is luxury living with a large home, nights on the town, fur coats and fast cars (**F**).

©DIAGRAM

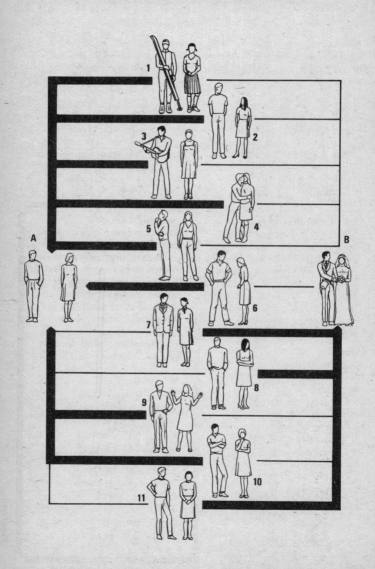

# Attraction and courtship

**Marriage factors** (*left*)
This diagram shows the results of a US study into the effect of various personality factors on mate selection (R. Sindberg et al, 1972). In the study were 25 couples who had married after a computer introduction; all the people involved had had earlier unsuccessful pairings within the same group. The fact that all people in the study were matched for age, race, social class, education and religion suggested that the success or failure of introductions was influenced by a number of other factors as follows.

**A Less often married**
1 One partner very much more interested in sport.
2 One partner very much taller.
3 Man more interested in fine art and music.
4 Man in need of more affection.
5 Man's thinking more abstract.
6 One very dominant: other very submissive.
9 One very undisciplined: other very controlled.
10 Man much more tense.
**B More often married**
7 Couple similarly sober or happy-go-lucky.
8 Couple similarly confident or apprehensive.
11 One witty: other placid.

**Vive la difference?** (*below*)
A Californian study (R. Centers, 1972) asked male and female students to rate the qualities they thought most important in men and in women. Our box lists the top ten qualities for each sex. Obviously these students were little influenced by the current blurring of gender roles — their "ideal" persons closely resemble traditional sex stereotypes.

**Men**
1 Achievement.
2 Leadership.
3 Occupational ability.
4 Economic ability.
5 Entertaining ability.
6 Intellectual ability.
7 Observational ability.
8 Common sense.
9 Athletic ability.
10 Theoretical ability.

**Women**
1 Physical attractiveness.
2 Erotic ability.
3 Affectional ability.
4 Social ability.
5 Domestic ability.
6 Sartorial ability.
7 Interpersonal understanding.
8 Art appreciation.
9 Moral-spiritual understanding.
10 Art-creative ability.

©DIAGRAM

# Finding a partner 1

Romantic plots in literature and movies tend to suggest that loving couples are in some miraculous way drawn together against the most amazing odds. In practice, however, some rather more mundane considerations are generally involved in determining who is likely to meet and ultimately to marry whom.

Propinquity — or residential proximity — remains an important factor in finding a partner. Marriage to the girl or boy "next door" may be less common than it was, but research suggests that the majority of people still marry someone from the same city if not from the same neighborhood as themselves. Of the increasing numbers of young people who now leave their parental homes to live in other parts of the country for reasons of education or employment, the majority can be expected to marry someone who shares their new place of residence. People who live near one another are statistically much more likely to meet, whether in the street, at educational institutions, at work, at parties, discos or bars, or through mutual friends. Once they have met, couples who live close to each other usually find it easier to establish a long-term relationship than do couples who, for example, meet on vacation and have homes that are hundreds of miles apart.

Another major factor in finding a partner is what is termed homogamy — the marrying of like with like. The degree of "likeness" obviously varies from couple to couple, and in some respects, particularly as regards personality traits, there appears to be more truth in the old adage that "opposites attract." Characteristics for which homogamy does appear to be influential in the finding of a partner include age and social background. Most people marry someone who is approximately the same age as themselves and most choose someone of similar background. In both cases this probably results partly from the basic attraction process and partly from social conditioning.

## Age and marriage

Most people marry someone close to their own age (**A**). Usually the age difference is less than five years and usually the man is older than the woman. In marriages with a big difference in age it is much more common for the man to be older than the woman (**B**) than for the woman to be older than the man (**C**).

## Propinquity and marriage

A sample 232 couples of varying backgrounds married in Bristol, UK in 1973-74 are here compared for premarital propinquity.

**a** Same district 18%.
**b** Adjacent districts 13%.
**c** Same quarter 14%.
**d** Different quarters 35%.
**e** Only one from Bristol 13%.
**f** Neither from Bristol 2%.
**g** No information 5%.

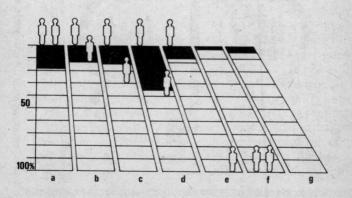

# Finding a partner 2

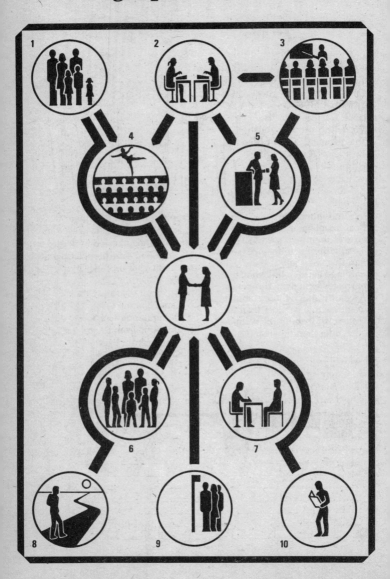

# Attraction and courtship

**How people meet**

People find their partners in a wide variety of ways, some of which are illustrated here.

**1** Family gatherings: meetings with distant relatives or the friends of family friends.

**2** Work: forming relationships with colleagues or their friends.

**3** Further education: full- or part-time study for career advancement or pleasure.

**4** Leisure activities: theater, ballet, concerts, dancing, exhibitions and sports.

**5** Social gatherings: parties, bars, pubs and evenings spent with friends.

**6** Community action: church, local politics, helping with charities or youth groups.

**7** Dating and marriage bureaus: introductions to likely partners chosen by computer or by experienced personnel.

**8** Travel: tourist resorts, holidays for people with shared interests or for young singles.

**9** Chance encounters: at a bus stop, in a supermarket line, at the laundromat — in fact the possibilities are endless.

**10** Advertisements: "lonely hearts" columns in newspapers or magazines.

© DIAGRAM

# Courtship 1

There are two broad types of courtship ritual: social rituals entered upon as a preliminary to marriage, and a mating ritual that serves to prepare a couple for sexual intercourse. The social rituals of courtship vary from culture to culture and from period to period. The mating ritual, however, is an integral part of the procreative process and is thus basically similar for everyone.

Although arranged marriages still remain the rule in some parts of the world — notably in India, Japan and the Arab world — most people in the West now have the pleasures and also the responsibilities of finding their own marriage partners. This personal selection process may not be as ritualized as, for example, the formal introduction of a prospective Japanese couple, but a typical modern Western courtship is not without its own customs associated with making each other's acquaintance, dating, and being introduced to the other person's family.

The physical ritual by which humans prepare to mate typically consists of an easily recognizable series of progressively more intimate actions. The complexity of this typical pattern is believed by some scientists to have been an important element in the establishment of long-term human partnerships for the rearing of children.

# Attraction and courtship

**Encouragement and repulsion**
When two people talk together their attitude toward each other is signaled by many small body movements. Keyed into our illustration are some common examples of signals indicating encouragement (**1**) and repulsion (**2**). Often the person making the movements has no recollection of doing so, and only sometimes is the other person consciously aware of them. Despite the mainly subconscious level on which these non-verbal forms of communication operate, most people are generally pretty quick to get the other's message!

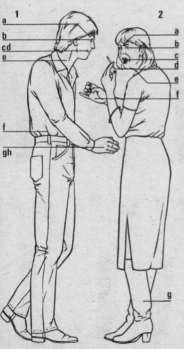

**1 Signals of encouragement**
**a** Eyebrows raised.
**b** Eyes wide open, pupils dilated, prolonged eye-contact.
**c** Mouth open and smiling.
**d** Lips moistened more often with tongue.
**e** Nods head in agreement.
**f** Body inclined toward other person.
**g** Expressive hand gestures.
**h** Small touching movements.

**2 Signals of repulsion**
**a** Frowns.
**b** Cold stare, pupils not dilated, looks away and appears to be disinterested.
**c** Sneers, yawns, pouts.
**d** Chain smokes.
**e** Shakes head in disagreement.
**f** Fidgets, cracks fingers, picks nails or teeth.
**g** Moves away from other person.

©DIAGRAM

# Courtship 2

**Mating ritual**
Although people get to know each other in different ways and at different rates, the physical actions that serve to mark and also to further their increasing intimacy tend to correspond to the general pattern shown by these illustrations.

**1** Eye to body — couple look at each other's face and body but avoid eye contact.
**2** Eye to eye — couple become aware of mutual interest and catch each other's eye.
**3** Voice to voice — couple talk and compare ideas. If these are similar the pattern will probably continue, but if there is a marked personality clash the relationship may end here.

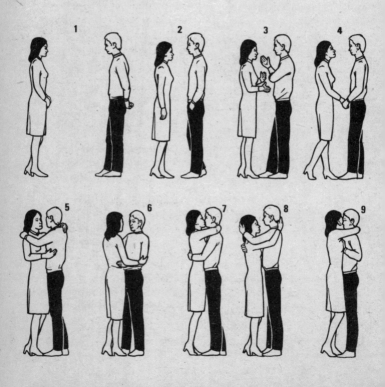

**4** Hand to hand — this first touch may be incorporated into another movement such as handing an object to the other person.

**5** Arm to shoulder — bodies are brought closer together. This action may also be disguised as another kind of movement.

**6** Arm to waist — bodies in close contact, a more intimate stage that may be reached prematurely if the couple dance together.

**7** Mouth to mouth — the kiss, which often marks the start of foreplay and the first serious sexual contact. The traditional "good-night kiss," often of little significance to either partner, may occur much earlier.

**8** Hand to head — this stage indicates a growing trust between the couple as they continue to kiss and begin to caress each other's face and hair.

**9** Hand to body — couple begin to explore, stroke and caress each other's body. This is the pre-copulatory stage, and if passed will probably be followed by sexual intercourse.

**10** Mouth to breast — more intimate body contact that often precedes sexual intercourse. Now in private and without clothing, the couple continue to kiss and embrace each other.

**11** Hand to genitals — hands are used to stimulate and explore each other's genitals. Sometimes the couple proceed to oral-genital stimulation.

**12** Genitals to genitals — the final stage. The man's penis enters the woman's vagina and sexual intercourse takes place.

# Chapter 5

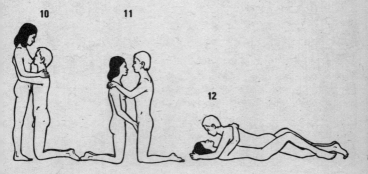

# The sexual process

Part of an engraving by Rembrandt of a couple making love, 1646.

# Arousal 1

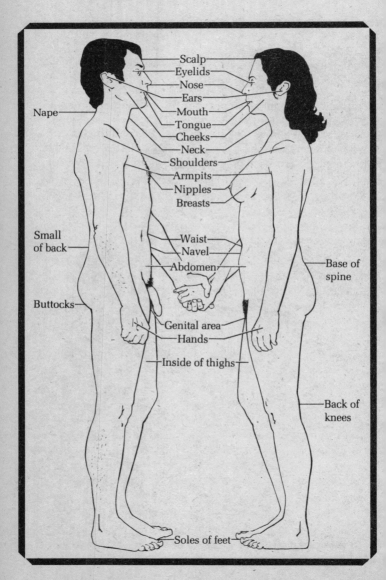

Scalp
Eyelids
Nose
Ears
Mouth
Tongue
Cheeks
Neck
Shoulders
Armpits
Nipples
Breasts

Nape

Small of back

Buttocks

Waist
Navel
Abdomen

Base of spine

Genital area
Hands

Inside of thighs

Back of knees

Soles of feet

# The sexual process

Sexual arousal is a set of physical responses making a male or female ready for intercourse. A wide range of stimuli may bring this about. Arousal can be a result of reflex nerve responses to stimulation of parts of the skin rich in nerve endings. The most sensitive of these so-called erogenous zones are the genitals, abdomen, buttocks and thighs. A woman's most responsive area is the clitoris; a man's is the lower side of the head of the penis. Lips, tongue, eyes, nose, nipples and breasts are other very sensitive places. Touching, stroking, kissing or even blowing on one or more erogenous zones may cause the penis or clitoris to erect.

**Erogenous zones**
Individual responses vary, but for most people stimulation by hand or mouth of the erogenous zones indicated here is most likely to result in sexual arousal.

# Arousal 2

Because the supply of nerve endings to, say, lips or nose, varies with individuals, some people find those parts of the body less sensitive than others do. But regular manipulation of even non-erogenous parts of the body can cause arousal simply because the recipient learns to associate this activity with sexual intercourse. The order in which someone stimulates different areas of the partner's body is important in achieving arousal.

Arousal can also come indirectly, through a stimulus perceived by the eyes or nose, or even from the very idea of sexual activity. Viewing erotic films or books or sharing erotic fantasies with a partner may stimulate sexual desire. (Few, if any, aphrodisiacs truly do that, although alcohol removes inhibitions.) Indirect stimuli trigger nerve impulses via the brain to the lower spinal column where nerve centers stimulate the sex organs.

The arousing effects of direct or indirect stimulation may be canceled by mood change or outside interruption.

**Kissing**
As partners grow more intimate lip-to-lip kissing may give way to deep kissing, with the tongue of one partner probing the open mouth of the other. This may send nerve signals from the tongue via the fifth cranial nerve to the entire nervous system so that spine, adrenal glands, pancreas and pelvic nerve endings go into action in various ways.

# The sexual process

## Male arousal

Signals from splanchnic nerves supplying the genitals cause the dorsal artery of the penis (**1**) to widen. This lets extra blood into the spongy cylinders of the penis (**2**) so they swell. This swelling squeezes the veins that carry blood from the penis (**3**) so that blood gets trapped in the penis, making it swell even more. The dartos muscle (**4**) contracts, shrinking the scrotum by crinkling its skin. Cremaster muscles (**5**) contract, pulling the testes in toward the rest of the body. Cowper's glands (**6**) yield mucus that lubricates the foreskin (**7**). These genital changes accompany changes in breathing and blood supply that between them affect all parts of the body.

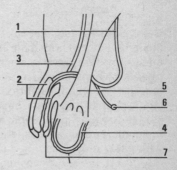

## Female arousal

Signals sent out from pudendal nerves cause erection of the spongy tissues in the clitoris (**a**) and in bulbs (**b**) on each side of the vaginal opening. The swelling of these bulbs produces the so-called orgasmic platform (p.108). Glands opening into the cleft between the labia minora (**c**) help to lubricate the vaginal barrel with mucus.

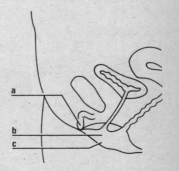

©DIAGRAM

# Phases of intercourse 1

Before, during and after sexual intercourse, measurable changes occur in both male and female sex organs. These alterations take place in stages corresponding to the four phases involved in sexual intercourse: excitement, plateau level, orgasm, and resolution. The main functions of these changes up to and including orgasm are: making the penis able to penetrate the vagina; making the vagina receptive to the penis; and releasing sperm when the penis is positioned where it is most likely to fertilize an ovum. During resolution, the sex organs return to normal.

**Phases of intercourse**
Present knowledge of the four phases occurring during sexual intercourse — excitement, plateau, orgasm and resolution — and of the bodily changes that accompany them come largely from work in the 1960s by William H. Masters and Virginia E. Johnson. Their *Human Sexual Response* is a basis for much of the material presented here.

**Changes to sex organs**
Stylized diagrams on the next four pages show changes to male and female sex organs during the four phases of sexual intercourse. Our diagrams are for a couple using the intercourse position illustrated *below*, with the man on top and the woman's knees raised, but the physiological changes are the same whatever position is used.

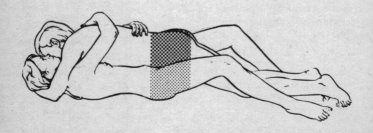

## Excitement phase:

**In males** Sexual arousal automatically sends blood into the three cylinder-shaped spongy masses in the penis (**1**). This swells, stiffens, lengthens and juts out from the body. Muscular contraction makes the scrotal sac rise slightly (**2**) and draws the testes upward (**3**). If the excitement phase exceeds 5-10 minutes, the scrotal sac and testes may descend. Penile erection may be lost if sexual stimulus is countered by such things as fear or sudden noise; or lost and regained repeatedly if sexual stimulus wanes and waxes.

**In females** The vaginal wall sweats droplets that coat and lubricate the vaginal barrel (**a**). The wall also turns purplish. The vagina dilates and the inner two-thirds of the barrel widens and lengthens (**b**). Meanwhile the uterus rises in the pelvis (**c**) and the cervix is pulled up away from the vagina. The labia majora (outer lips) open and may flatten out (**d**). The labia minora (inner lips) thicken and thrust outward. The clitoris lengthens and thickens (**e**).

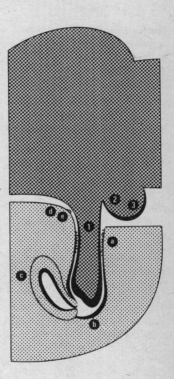

©DIAGRAM

# Phases of intercourse 2

**Plateau phase:**

**In males**  The penis may grow slightly larger near its tip, whose reddish-purple color often deepens (**4**). Two or three drops of mucus now come from the opening at the tip (**5**). The testes are drawn higher still and may become enlarged by half as much again (**6**).

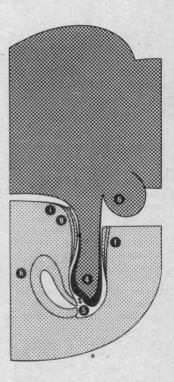

**In females**  The outer one-third of the vagina thickens as more blood flows to it (**f**). This narrows the barrel cavity, and muscular contraction makes the vagina grip the penis here. (The swollen outer vagina and labia minora form a long, so-called orgasmic platform (**g**).) Meanwhile the labia minora go from pink to red, or from red to deep red in women who have had babies. The labia majora may continue swelling. The uterus continues rising (**h**). The clitoris pulls back beneath its hood of skin (**i**).

**Orgasm phase:**

**In males** A series of swift, involuntary rhythmic muscular contractions in the penis (**7**), testes (**8**), and nearby areas force semen (**9**) from the penis. The first three or four contractions occur at 0.8-second intervals. Their forceful ejaculations can squirt semen as much as 2ft.

**In females** The orgasmic platform contracts rhythmically 3-15 times at 0.8-second intervals, with decreasing intensity (**j**). Contractions also happen in the uterus (**k**). Labia majora, labia minora and clitoris show no known changes during orgasm.

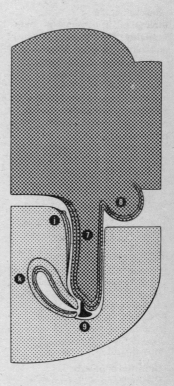

# Phases of intercourse 3

**Resolution phase**
**In males** The resolution phase consists of two stages. The penis quickly shrinks to half its fully erect size (**10**). Reduction to normal size takes longer. Keeping the penis in the partner's vagina prolongs this process. As the penis shrinks, the scrotum becomes looser (**11**) and the testes descend again (**12**).
**In females** The clitoris returns to its normal position (**l**) by 10 seconds after vaginal contractions stop. The entire vagina may take 15 minutes to return to normal color, size and position (**m**). Research by Masters and Johnson suggested that the uterus might take around 20 minutes to return to normal (**n**). Labia majora (**o**) take up to 3 hours in mothers. Labia minora may revert from red to pink in 10 seconds.

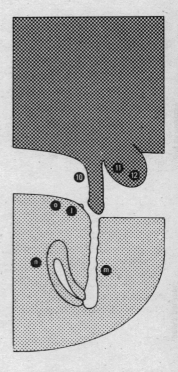

**Duration of phases**
Excitement may last minutes or hours depending on techniques used and lack of distraction. The plateau phase is brief and intense. Orgasm is shortest of all: a mere few seconds. Many of the changes in resolution are over in 10 minutes. New stimulation will arouse most women just after intercourse, but most men have a refractory period when restimulation is impossible.

**Intensity of phases** (right)
By measuring such things as penile erection, vaginal blood volume, blood pressure, heart rate and breathing rate scientists are able to compare the intensity of bodily response during the different phases of intercourse. Our three graphs show bodily changes during excitement (**a**), the plateau phase (**b**), orgasm (**c**) and resolution (**d**).

# The sexual process

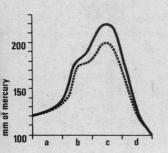

### Blood pressure
During intercourse, a woman's systolic blood pressure (pressure caused by contracting heart muscle) rises from 120mm of mercury possibly to 175mm in the plateau phase and even to 200mm in orgasm. A man's blood pressure may rise even more: to 180mm in the plateau phase, and to 220mm at orgasm. Then pressure soon returns to normal.

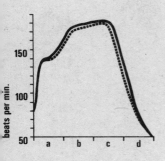

### Heart rate
The rate at which the heart beats may increase relatively more than the rise in blood pressure. By the plateau phase a woman's heart rate may have more than doubled: from a normal 80 beats per minute up to 175, although 140 is the median. In orgasm the rate goes even higher. A man's rate rises similarly, and may touch 180 in orgasm.

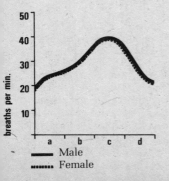

— Male
•••••• Female

### Breathing rate
Both sexes breathe faster and louder as sexual tension builds up during intercourse. This so-called heavy breathing becomes noticeable in the plateau phase. At orgasm men and women may be taking 40 breaths per minute — twice the normal number. Like blood pressure and heart rate, respiration rate soon returns to normal after orgasm.

# Other responses 1

As already described (pages 106-111), the four phases of intercourse are characterized by significant changes to the male and female sex organs and by marked increases in blood pressure, heart rate and breathing rate as orgasm approaches. Here we look at four other types of bodily response occurring during intercourse — the appearance of a sex flush, the swelling of different parts of the body, the build up and release of muscle tension, and the incidence of perspiration. Sex flush and perspiration occur only in some men and women: swelling and muscle tension are experienced by everyone.

**Sex flush in men (1)**
Only 25% of men experience a sex flush during intercourse. Onset is late in the excitement phase or during the plateau phase. The flush starts on the stomach and then moves to the chest, neck and face. The flush disappears within 5 minutes of orgasm.

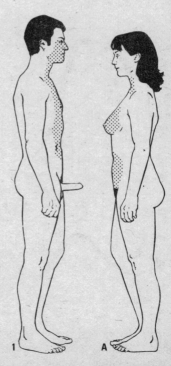

**Sex flush in women (A)**
In the excitement phase 75% of women develop a skin rash on the abdomen and throat, spreading to the breasts. Intensity relates to sexual stimulation but rises in the plateau phase. The measles-like rash fades within 5 minutes of orgasm.

# The sexual process

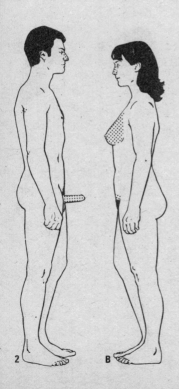

### Swelling in men (2)
Swelling of the penis and testes has already been described. In addition, the walls of a man's inner nose swell as the surface blood circulation increases and more blood enters distensible areas through arteries than can escape from the fine network of capillaries and on through veins.

### Swelling in women (B)
Apart from genital swelling (see earlier), breasts and walls of the inner nose swell as more blood enters than can leave. By the plateau phase, areolae (dark rings around the nipples) engulf the nipples, and breasts reach maximum size. They take up to 10 minutes to subside after orgasm.

©DIAGRAM

# Other responses 2

**Muscle tension in men (3)**
Late in the excitement phase muscles erect the nipples of six in 10 men, and voluntary muscular contractions occur in arms, legs and abdomen. In the plateau phase involuntary clawing and grimacing may occur, toes curl and feet arch. In orgasm contractions affect sphincter muscles in the rectum. Muscular tension fades within 5 minutes of orgasm.

**Muscle tension in women (C)**
Muscles in pelvis, abdomen, back and thighs contract and nipples grow erect. In the plateau phase muscle tension produces tense thighs, arched back, rigid neck, flared nostrils, grimacing, and clawing hands and feet. Muscle spasms accompany orgasm but tension goes within 5 minutes.

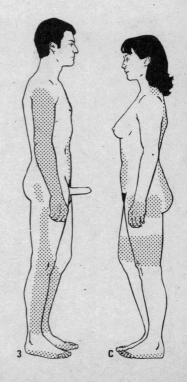

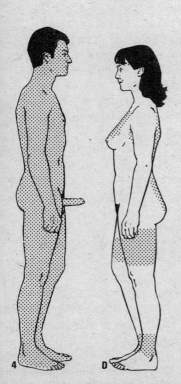

**Perspiration in men (4)**
One man in three perspires as
soon as orgasm is over. Usually
only the hands and feet perspire
but sometimes the entire body
may be involved.

**Perspiration in women (D)**
After orgasm one woman in three
may perspire freely under the
arms and on the forehead and
top lip. Perspiration may also
thinly cover her back, chest,
thighs and ankles.

©DIAGRAM

# Orgasm 1

The irritation and spasm occurring at this peak of sexual activity have been likened to a sneeze. But no other bodily process produces such intense sensations of excitement or emotional release. Not just the genitals but the whole body's muscles and nervous system are involved. Women have described orgasm as starting with a momentary feeling of suspension. Then an intense sensual feeling spreads up from the clitoris. Senses of hearing, taste and vision are briefly weakened or lost. Next, warmth floods from the pelvic area throughout the body. Lastly, the vaginal area begins to throb.

Orgasm produces similar sensations in men. Incidentally because some men and women can reach orgasm by fantasy alone, the idea that there are different (clitoral, vaginal, penile) kinds of orgasm is a fallacy.

Orgasm usually lasts 3-10 seconds, but up to 1 minute in some women. Duration, intensity and pleasure all vary from one sex act to another.

The diagrams on these pages detail the sexual events involved. (See also pages 106-111.)

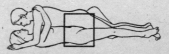

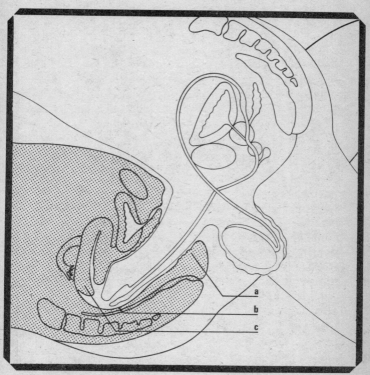

a
b
c

## Orgasm in women

The sensations accompanying orgasm are as intense for women as for men. But the fluid that sometimes spurts from the vagina in orgasm is not true ejaculate as some believe: simply lubricant escaping as the vaginal muscles suddenly contract. During orgasm the orgasmic platform (**a**) — largely the outer part of the vaginal barrel — rhythmically contracts from 3 to 15 times. A large number of strong contractions produces a more powerful orgasm than a few weak ones. The inner "blind" end of the vagina (**b**) grows longer and wider. As it rises from the vagina, the uterus (**c**) produces a tenting effect. Meanwhile the uterus rhythmically contracts.

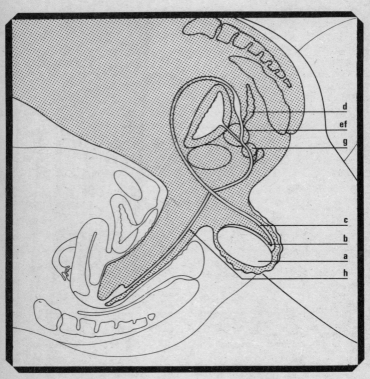

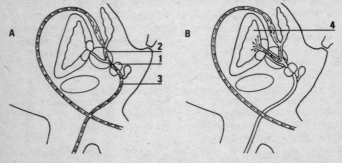

### Orgasm in men

The major difference between male and female orgasm is that males emit and ejaculate sperm and females do not.

**Emission** Waves of contractions in smooth muscle pass through the testes (**a**), epididymides (**b**) and vasa deferentia (**c**). They also affect the seminal vesicles (**d**). Accordingly seminal fluid and sperm collect in ejaculatory ducts (**e**) inside the prostate gland (**f**). Compressor muscles (**g**) relax and let semen into the urethra (**h**). As the emission phase begins, men get a feeling that ejaculation is inevitable and nothing they could do would stop it.

**Ejaculation** The prostate's pumping action and muscular contractions that affect the urethra send semen spurting through the urethra and from the penis. Most semen is ejaculated by the first five or six contractions.

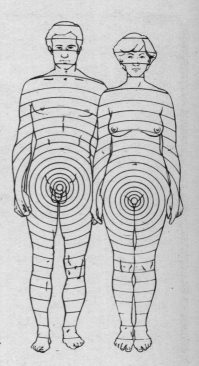

### A) Normal ejaculation

Compressor muscles (**1**) relax to let seminal fluid out of the prostate (**2**) into the urethra (**3**) for discharge through the penis.

### B) Retrograde ejaculation

In this abnormality, which may result from prostate surgery or an accident, the compressor muscles fail to relax and seminal fluid is discharged into the bladder (**4**).

### Orgasmic waves

In both sexes, the experience of orgasm is centered in the pelvic region: in a man's penis, prostate and seminal vesicles, and in a woman's clitoris, vagina and uterus. Intense sensations associated with orgasm, however, are felt, often as a flood of intense pleasure, throughout the entire body.

©DIAGRAM

# Conception 1

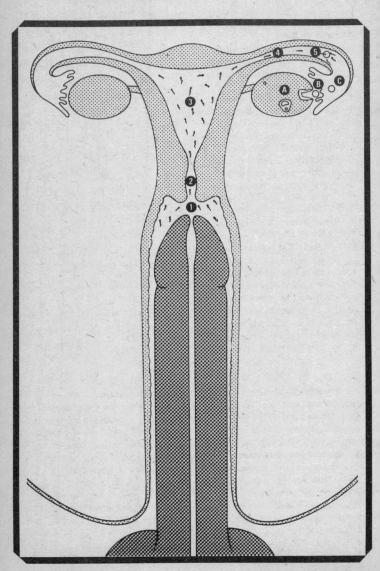

Conception (the start of a new life) happens when an egg in a woman's Fallopian tube is invaded by a sperm. The process by which they meet is complex and ingenious. Early in the (monthly) menstrual cycle a new egg begins maturing in a follicle in one ovary. At mid-cycle the follicle bursts and frees the egg — an event called ovulation. By day 14 the endometrium (uterine lining) thickens, ready to receive the egg if this is fertilized. Meanwhile the egg enters the woman's peritoneal cavity, where "tentacles" around one end of a Fallopian tube capture it and feed the egg into the tube. Hairs lining the tube's inner walls help to beat the

**Sperm meets egg**
This diagram plots the progress of egg and sperm inside the female reproductive tract to the point where sperm meets egg and conception can occur.
**A** Egg still in ovary.
**B** Egg enters peritoneal cavity.
**C** Egg in Fallopian tube.
**1** Sperm enter vagina.
**2** Sperm in cervix.
**3** Sperm in uterus.
**4** Sperm in Fallopian tube.
**5** Sperm meets egg.

©DIAGRAM

# Conception 2

egg along toward the uterus.

If intercourse happens at about this time the egg may be fertilized. At orgasm, the man's penis ejaculates on average 480 million sperm into the woman's vagina. Most perish in the 1- to 5-hour journey up through the woman's reproductive tract. Acid conditions inside the vagina kill off half the sperm. The rest enter the cervix where they readily pass through the normally impenetrable mucus, thanks to changes caused by ovulation. Sperm swim on into

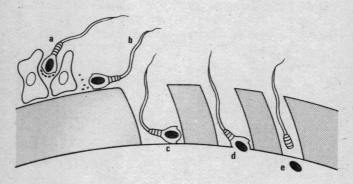

**Fertilization**

Fertilization occurs when the nucleus of a sperm invades an egg. For this to happen the sperm must have matured inside the male reproductive system. Also the sperm head's outer "skin" must be modified so that the sperm can penetrate the egg. This so-called capacitation takes place on the journey through the female reproductive tract.

**a** A sperm releases an enzyme that helps it burrow between cells surrounding the egg.
**b** The outer "skin" of the sperm head disintegrates, and the head binds onto the egg's protective outer zone.
**c** The enzyme acrosin helps the sperm tunnel through this zone.
**d** The sperm fuses with the egg.
**e** The sperm nucleus enters the egg as the sperm's tail drops off.

the uterus, moving at up to 1 inch in 8 minutes. But their main impetus comes from the contracting uterine muscle: dead sperm travel as fast as live ones.

Only about 3000 sperm reach the Fallopian tube that holds the egg. Of this already greatly diminished total, a mere few hundred will actually reach the egg and usually only one will penetrate and fertilize it to conceive a new life. Conception is possible if sperm enter the vagina from three days before ovulation to one day after.

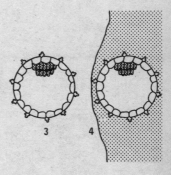

### From egg to embryo

Once a sperm has fertilized an egg, changes to the surface of the egg shut out other sperm.

**1** In one day the zygote (the fertilized egg) divides in two.

**2** After four days the dividing cells form a ball of cells called a morula, from the Latin for "mulberry." This gets pushed down its Fallopian tube and on into the uterus.

**3** After seven days the morula turns into a hollow ball called a blastocyst. Its outer cells form a wall called a trophoblast. Inside is a fluid-filled yolk sac and clustered inner cells.

**4** The blastocyst sinks into the uterus lining. This nourishes the specializing inner cells. In a month they multiply to form an embryo 10,000 times larger than the egg they came from.

# Chapter 6

Erotic illustrations from a deck of
Indian playing cards.

# Sexual intercourse

# The act of intercourse 1

Sexual intercourse is a biological reproduction device with uniquely sensual pleasure built in to motivate and reward the couple taking part. For most partners on most occasions, however, the aim of the sex act is not to produce children but to enjoy physical closeness and to express their love for each other. Advances in birth control, by largely removing the risks of unwanted pregnancy, have added enormously to this element of pleasure.

The sexual act has countless variations, and couples bring to it their own preferences and techniques. These can involve foreplay, intercourse, orgasm, and postcoital activity – the whole sexual process.

**Foreplay** Besides stiffening the penis and relaxing and lubricating the vagina ready for entry, foreplay involves actions that are in themselves pleasurable. Typical are stroking, kissing, blowing, sucking and licking different parts of the partner's unclothed body.

**Intercourse** can start with the man thrusting his hips forward to push penis into vagina, or with the woman lowering her vagina onto the penis. It may proceed with the man on top (the usual American and European position) or with the woman on top (common elsewhere); standing or sitting; face-to-face or rear-entry; with interlocked legs or with one partner's legs inside or outside the other's. There are hundreds of variations, some so demanding that only accomplished gymnasts perform them. The following pages show just a few possibilities.

**Orgasm** Some couples aim at simultaneous orgasm. Others prefer to reach a climax in turn, or to have more than one orgasm each. Afterward the couple may just lie close together or may continue lovemaking, perhaps with an activity other than intercourse.

There are good reasons for exploring different sexual techniques. Variety stops the sex act growing routine and stale for regular partners. Both or one may gain particular pleasure from some unusual position. They may find they enjoy starting one way and shifting to other positions before reaching a climax. Then, too, what gives most pleasure may depend on the conditions in which a sex act takes place. The best position may depend for example on whether the room has a bed, whether the couple are hurried, or whether the man or woman feels tired.

Trying out new techniques can be fun, provided each partner sets out to please the other. In fact finding out and supplying what your partner enjoys most in bed is one of the surest ways of keeping together.

# The act of intercourse 2

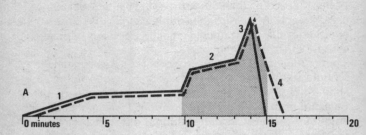

**Patterns of intercourse**
These diagrams illustrate four typical patterns of intercourse.
**A Mutual orgasm** Here the pattern of responses of the two partners is essentially the same — a progressive increase in sexual excitement culminates in almost simultaneous orgasm.

**B Brief intercourse** After only the briefest of preliminaries, intercourse begins and the man rapidly attains orgasm. Few women experience such immediate responses, and most obtain little or no satisfaction unless sexual activity is resumed.

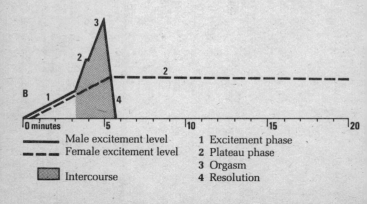

| | |
|---|---|
| —— Male excitement level | 1 Excitement phase |
| – – – Female excitement level | 2 Plateau phase |
| | 3 Orgasm |
| ▨ Intercourse | 4 Resolution |

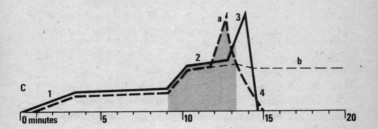

**C Withdrawal** Usually for purposes of contraception the man withdraws his penis just before ejaculation. Ideally the woman reaches orgasm (**a**) before this takes place, as she is otherwise likely to remain unsatisfied (**b**).

**D Prolonged intercourse** In the example illustrated, the woman has two orgasms before her partner experiences his own. In most cases this results from conscious control by the man, who may choose to slow down his own responses, perhaps by lying still for a time soon after entry.

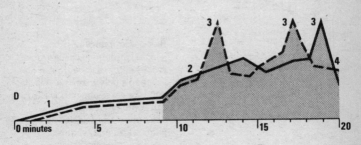

# Man-on-top positions 1

The commonest position is face to face with the man on top — often called the "missionary" or "matrimonial" position. Most women like this best. Until the later 1900s most American men used no other, and indeed some states ban many others as unnatural.

The missionary position is more adaptable than most others. Intercourse can be shallow, prolonged and tender; or deep, brief and tough. A couple may start with this position. To delay his orgasm they may shift to others as intercourse progresses, and then end with the missionary position as the one likeliest to produce mutual orgasm.

**Basic missionary position**
This position relaxes the woman, makes entry easy, and promotes the man's pelvic thrusts. It is also good for caressing and kissing. But some women suffer discomfort from deep penetration and want more freedom to move. This position is not good if he is heavy or suffers premature ejaculation, or if she is in late pregnancy.

## Man-on-top positions

**1** The man supports his upper body with his arms so the woman need not bear all his weight. After entry she closes her legs so her vagina grips his penis.
**2** She keeps both legs open.
**3** She lifts one leg. He supports himself as in (**1**) and (**2**).

**4** The woman raises both legs, to deepen penetration. The man supports himself on forearms only, for a closer embrace.
**5** The woman holds her ankles to keep her knees sharply drawn up for even deeper penetration.

©DIAGRAM

# Man-on-top positions 2

**Man-on-top positions**
**6** The woman curls one leg over her partner.
**7** She raises both legs outside her partner and presses one leg against the other.
**8** She lifts one leg high.
**9** She lifts both legs high — a deep-penetration position.
**10** He leans on his hands as she lifts both legs and supports her thighs.

**11** He lies half raised. She lies with legs up and knees bent.
**12** He kneels on one leg. She lifts her leg on that side.
**13** He kneels on one leg and she lifts both legs high.
**14** He kneels with legs outside hers, which remain straight.
**15** He kneels and supports her raised body with his hands.

©DIAGRAM

133

# Woman-on-top positions 1

The opposite of the missionary position is face-to-face with the woman astride. This leaves her free to control length and intensity of intercourse. She can also start kneeling and shift to lying or other positions without losing contact. Some sexologists claim that "woman astride" gives the greatest pleasure for both partners. By the mid 1970s most couples had at least tried it.

**Woman on top**
This way she can make pelvic thrusts and determine depth of penetration, free from the man's weight. He is free to caress and can often delay orgasm. This position is good if he is tall and she is short. But clumsy insertion while squatting can injure; he may dislike a passive role; and the method is poor for achieving conception.

## Woman-on-top positions

**1** The couple lie in an embrace with the woman's legs inside the man's.

**2** The woman supports herself on her hands and the man pulls her hips toward him.

**3** This position is like (**2**) but he lies with legs together and she spreads hers apart.

**4** Half kneeling, half lying assures shallow penetration.

**5** She kneels close to him to secure deep penetration combined with a close embrace.

# Woman-on-top positions 2

## Woman-on-top positions

**6** This way the couple keep eye contact during deep penetration.
**7** This position lets him easily stimulate her clitoris by hand.
**8** She squats astride him. If she has good vulval muscle control she may bring him to orgasm without pelvic thrusting.

**9** She leans back, propped up by her hands.
**10** She leans back and he sits up, with hands as supports.
**11** She sits on one of his thighs, partly propped up by the other.

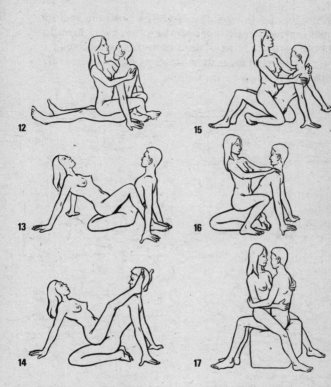

**12** She sits with legs wrapped around his back.
**13** She leans back and he sits in a cross-legged position.
**14** She leans back with legs on his shoulders; he kneels.

**15** She kneels and his knees are half bent. Bent even more they could support her back.
**16** She sits on his thighs and he kneels as in (**14**).
**17** Both partners sit face-to-face, she on his thighs.

©DIAGRAM

137

# Side-by-side positions

Advantages of side-by-side intercourse positions include the fact that neither partner bears the other's weight and also that both partners have all their limbs free for embrace. But some couples find them unsatisfactory because they offer insufficient scope for stimulation.

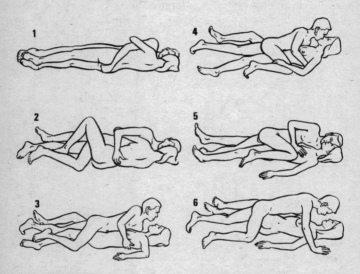

**Side-by-side positions**

**1** The couple lie on their sides in a close embrace, each keeping their legs together.
**2** Both partners lie on their sides, she with her legs apart outside his legs.
**3** She turns slightly to the side. He lies partly on top of her, with one of his legs between hers to give increased clitoral stimulation.

**4** This resembles (**3**) but he brings one knee forward.
**5** She lies on her back while he lies on his side with one leg over her.
**6** Lying on her back, she twists her buttocks to the side. He lies partly on top of her and makes a rear entry.

# Standing positions

Standing intercourse is often hasty, surreptitious and uncomfortable. Even when it is leisurely, there are problems to be solved if the partners are of unequal height. Some positions involve the man lifting the woman off the ground; this gets over difficulties relating to height but may make the man's muscles ache. Another solution is for a short partner to stand on an object such as a large book.

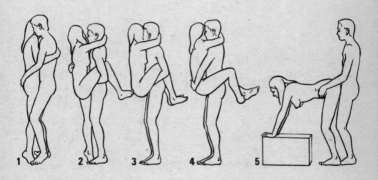

**Standing positions**

**1** The couple embrace, standing face to face. This works only if heights are roughly equal.

**2** He lifts one of her legs and can fondle her clitoris.

**3** He holds her off the ground, gripping her legs. She puts both arms around his neck.

**4** This is similar to (**3**), but she crosses her legs behind his back as he holds her lower back.

**5** For this rear-entry position, he stands upright as she leans forward with her hands on a low piece of furniture.

# Rear-entry positions 1

Many people think rear-entry intercourse unnatural. Yet almost all mammals only use this way. Rear entry offers satisfying deep penetration, and pleasing pressure on the clitoris. There are lying, kneeling, sitting and standing variants. Some are gentle, others vigorous. At least a few satisfy couples of all ages. Certain postures even suit people with medical conditions that rule out most other forms of intercourse.

**Rear entry**
Shown is an entry squarely from behind. Such positions can give a man stimulating buttock-body contact and let him fondle his partner's breasts, legs and clitoris. Kneeling gives deep penetration but needs care, for hard thrusting can cause pain and injury to ovaries. Lack of face-to-face contact is a snag with all rear-entry methods.

# Sexual intercourse

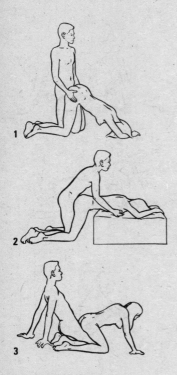

**1**

**2**

**4**

**3**

**5**

## Rear-entry positions

**1** He kneels upright, with legs together. She kneels head down, with legs apart.

**2** This position resembles (**1**) but this time she supports her upper body on a bed.

**3** She kneels, leaning forward. He kneels, leaning back. A snag of postures **3-10** is that they give him no scope for embracing; showing tenderness is vital if

intercourse is to express an emotional relationship.

**4** He kneels as in (**3**) while she squats on his thighs.

**5** He kneels as in (**3**). She kneels with upper body upright.

©DIAGRAM

141

# Rear-entry positions 2

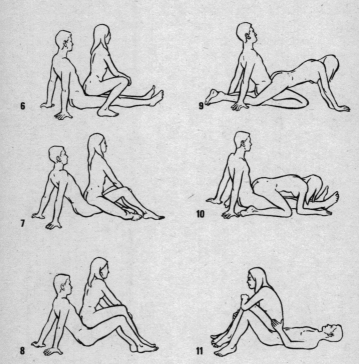

**Rear-entry positions**
**6** She squats and he sits with his legs extended.
**7** She sits with thighs spread, and grasps his raised knees.
**8** She sits with buttocks, thighs, legs and feet on him.

**9** She kneels with legs extended — a semi "wheelbarrow" position.
**10** He sits. She crouches.
**11** He lies legs apart. She sits between them.

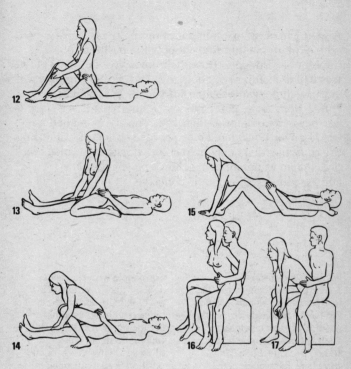

**12** He lies legs together. She straddles them.
**13** He lies supine while she sits astride, legs tucked back.
**14** He lies supine. She squats.

**15** She leans forward between his legs.
**16,17** These seated versions give close contact and very deep penetration. But this can hurt or harm the woman unless he exercises care.

©DIAGRAM

# Positions for special needs 1

A search for new, exciting sensations motivates most people who explore the hundreds of possible positions of intercourse. But apart from their novelty value, some of the less usual postures may help to solve a number of physical and psychological problems. If you are pregnant or fat, suffer from back pain, possess a short penis, or have a partner taller or shorter than you, a position you had not tried or even considered may prove to be the best. Choosing the right positions may help a non-orgasmic woman reach orgasm; an impotent man achieve potency; even a supposedly infertile couple conceive.

### Positions for virgins
**1** Many a first timer adopts the well-known missionary position. For male and female virgins the position matters less than the approach. This should be slow and considerate. Foreplay also stimulates lubrication of the vagina so that she feels little discomfort, especially if past petting has stretched or torn her hymen.

### Positions for conception
**2** She hooks her knees over his shoulders. This helps fat women win full penetration and semen to collect near the cervix.
**3** Rear-entry, kneeling, brings semen to cervix if the uterus is retroverted (tilted backward).

### For people with problems
**4** She squats over him. This position helps full penetration of women with tight vaginas.
**5** Side-by-side, facing, helps the ill, old, tired, tall-and-short.
**6** This side-by-side rear-entry position is recommended for men with a weak erection.
**7** This woman-on-top position is used in the treatment of male impotence (see p. 257) and premature ejaculation (p. 259). It is also used as a preliminary position in therapy for non-orgasmic women (p. 265).
**8** This side-by-side position makes uncontrolled hip movements easier for the woman and helps her reach orgasm; it is recommended as a follow-up to (7). (Also see p. 265.)

# Positions for special needs 2

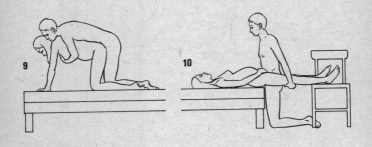

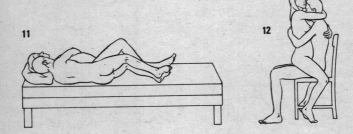

## Positions in pregnancy

Early in pregnancy a couple can have intercourse as usual unless a doctor bans intercourse in the first three months because of previous miscarriage. As her pregnancy advances and her waist thickens conventional intercourse grows awkward or impossible. She needs methods that avoid direct pressure on the abdomen or at least ones where she can control depth of penetration.

**9** Both partners kneel on a bed in a rear-entry position and he avoids overdeep thrusting.
**10** She lies legs apart with both ends of her body supported. Lack of abdominal pressure makes this suitable late in pregnancy.
**11** The couple lie side-by-side for rear entry. Again, there is no abdominal pressure.
**12** The couple embrace on a chair. She sits on his lap and so can control penetration.

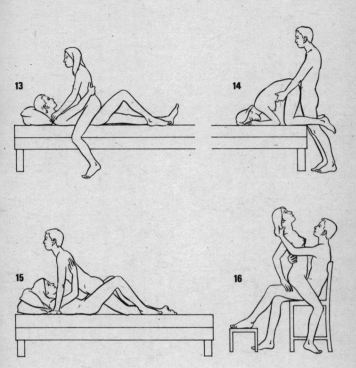

## For back pain sufferers

People subject to back pain may suffer excruciatingly in the conventional positions for intercourse. But there are often less usual positions that the victim can enjoy or at least tolerate. A considerate partner will try to find what these are. Four positions that are safe for most people with back pain are pictured here. In each case the pelvic thrusting should be left to the pain-free partner.

**13** He lies on a bed while she sits astride leaning forward. (He is the one with the pain.)
**14** He stands for rear-entry as she kneels face down on a bed. (He is the one with the pain.)
**15** She lies on a bed while he leans forward between her legs. (She is the one with the pain.)
**16** They sit face-to-face on a chair, she on his lap so she can do all the thrusting. (He is the one with the pain.)

©DIAGRAM

# Alternatives to intercourse 1

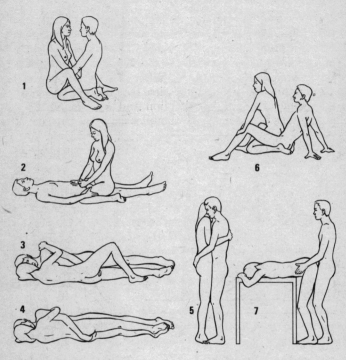

**Masturbation positions**

**1** She sits on the floor, legs gently apart. He kneels facing her so that each of them can at the same time masturbate the other.

**2** He lies back; she sits astride to masturbate him.

**3** The couple lie in an embrace and he masturbates her.

**Interfemoral sex positions**

In these, the man's penis is masturbated by the woman's thighs. Note they are not effective in avoiding conception: sperm may enter the vagina from the vulva.

**4** The couple lie side by side.

**5** The couple stand to embrace.

Lovemaking does not have to include penile-vaginal penetration. Many couples derive just as much pleasure from the other sexual activities described here. These can be enjoyed as specific alternatives to intercourse or may be incorporated into lovemaking before or after intercourse. Used as alternatives to intercourse they have the obvious advantage of avoiding conception, and are therefore sometimes recommended to couples using the rhythm method of birth control.

**Masturbation** is a common sexual activity among couples. It involves the erotic stimulation of the genitals by means other than sexual intercourse. Frequently used as an arousal technique, masturbation by one partner of the other can also be continued to orgasm. For maximum pleasure each partner should be aware of the other's preferences. For instance a woman manually masturbating a man should be aware of the speed of stroke and degree of pressure that he prefers; while he should remember that most women prefer pressure to be applied to the side of and around the clitoris rather than directly onto it.

**Anal sex,** in which the man's glans is inserted into his partner's rectum, is enjoyed by some couples as an alternative to conventional intercourse. Like oral-genital sex

**Positions for anal sex**
**6** While he sits legs stretched in front, she kneels head down facing his feet. He directs his penis to her rectum and then she bears down as he leans back.
**7** She leans over a table. He masturbates her clitoris as his penis enters her rectum.

©DIAGRAM

149

# Alternatives to intercourse 2

it is sometimes disapproved of and is illegal in some countries. Scientific opinion, however, is that there is nothing physically or psychologically wrong with it. Lubrication is recommended and there may still be slight or sometimes severe discomfort. To avoid the real risk of transferring germs, the man should never in the same act penetrate the woman's vagina after her rectum. Many counselors recommend that a condom be worn for anal sex.

**Oral-genital sex** is of two kinds. In cunnilingus a man uses his mouth to stimulate a woman's genitals; in fellatio a woman uses her mouth to stimulate a man's genitals. Techniques for each include kissing, licking, sucking and, in the case of fellatio, friction of the penis inside the woman's mouth. Oral-genital sex is sometimes disapproved of on the grounds that it is unnatural, unhygienic or simply "wrong." Its practice remains an offense on some statute books but prosecution is extremely unlikely and many people now accept oral-genital sex as a perfectly natural and enjoyable form of sexual activity. Women in particular can reach orgasm very easily in this way. Provided that the genitals are kept clean and healthy there are no valid objections to oral-genital sex on grounds of hygiene. Swallowing vaginal or seminal fluids is also harmless.

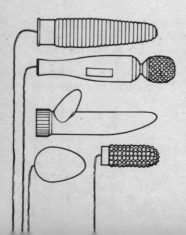

**Vibrators**
Vibrators can be used to give intense sexual pleasure, particularly to women. Some vibrators are penis-shaped and can be inserted into the vagina, but more usually vibrators are applied to the vulva or clitoris. Properly stimulated by a vibrator, few women fail to reach orgasm.

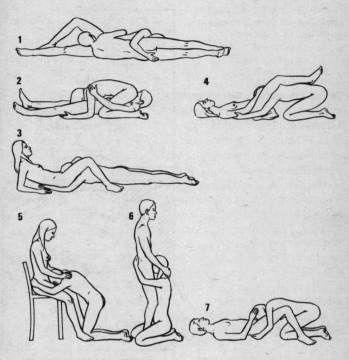

## Positions for oral-genital sex

1 The couple lie in the so-called "69" position, which allows his and her genitals to be stimulated simultaneously.

2 He lies on his back with his head raised. Facing his feet, she crouches over him to perform fellatio. He meanwhile performs cunnilingus.

3 She lies legs apart, head up to watch him perform cunnilingus as he lies between her legs.

4 With her buttocks supported on a cushion, she lies with her legs over his shoulders as he kneels to perform cunnilingus.

5 She sits on a chair with her legs slightly apart. He kneels to perform cunnilingus.

6 The woman kneels to perform fellatio as her partner stands. He meanwhile can stimulate her genitals with his feet.

7 He lies on his back with legs apart. She kneels between his legs to perform fellatio.

©DIAGRAM

# Chapter 7

1 Illustrations in comic-book style describing three common birth control methods.
2 A Hong Kong birth control poster appearing in *IPPF in Action 1980*, a pamphlet published by the International Planned Parenthood Federation.

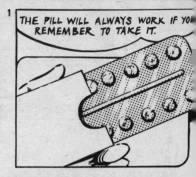

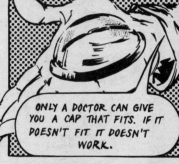

2

有計劃生育
免負擔困難

PLAN YOUR FAMILY
BEFORE IT'S TOO LATE

THE FAMILY PLANNING ASSOCIATION OF H.K.

香港家庭計劃指導會

香港會所：軒尼詩道一五二號
九龍會所：馬頭涌道一〇五號

# Birth control choices 1

Today, in Western countries at least, birth control is no longer the exception but the rule. In the United States approximately 80% of all couples use some form of contraception; for Western Europe the figure is about 70%. Despite this widespread use of contraception, however, many people are still uncertain about what methods of birth control are available, how efficient or safe each method is, and which particular method is most suitable for their own particular needs.

The main methods of birth control now in use are the pill, the intrauterine device (IUD), the cap, the condom, spermicides, withdrawal, the rhythm method, sterilization and abortion. Of these the pill, IUD, cap, sterilization and abortion need medical supervision, whereas the others do not.

Each method works by intercepting the process of conception at one or another of its stages. This may be by preventing ovulation (pill), by blocking the eggs' route through the Fallopian tubes (female sterilization), by preventing implantation (IUD), by acting as a barrier to or destroying sperm (cap, condom, spermicides), by preventing sperm from entering the vagina (withdrawal), or by abstaining from sex at certain times (rhythm method). Finally, abortion provides the means of deliberately terminating a pregnancy if conception has occurred.

The efficiency and safety of the various methods vary considerably. Unfortunately, the methods that are most effective also involve the most health risks. The combined pill is almost 100% effective, but health risks are significant particularly for women who are over 35, who smoke, or who have a family history of heart trouble. To a lesser extent, the minipill, IUD and female sterilization also carry health risks. Ultimately the choice of a contraceptive becomes a matter of balancing such health risks against the risk of producing an unwanted child.

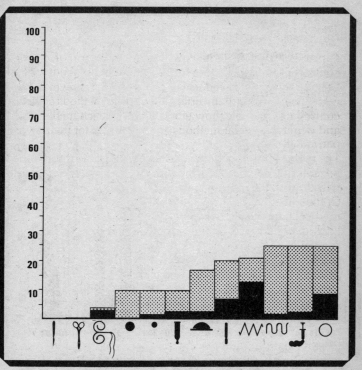

## Efficiency

Given here are failure rates for different types of contraception. Figures, based on US surveys, refer to pregnancies per 100 users during their first year of use. Theoretical rates are given first, with actual-use rates given in brackets wherever appropriate.

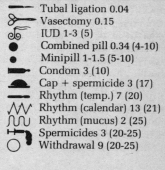

| | |
|---|---|
| Tubal ligation | 0.04 |
| Vasectomy | 0.15 |
| IUD | 1-3 (5) |
| Combined pill | 0.34 (4-10) |
| Minipill | 1-1.5 (5-10) |
| Condom | 3 (10) |
| Cap + spermicide | 3 (17) |
| Rhythm (temp.) | 7 (20) |
| Rhythm (calendar) | 13 (21) |
| Rhythm (mucus) | 2 (25) |
| Spermicides | 3 (20-25) |
| Withdrawal | 9 (20-25) |

■ Theoretical failure rate

▨ Actual-use failure rate

©DIAGRAM

# Birth control choices 2

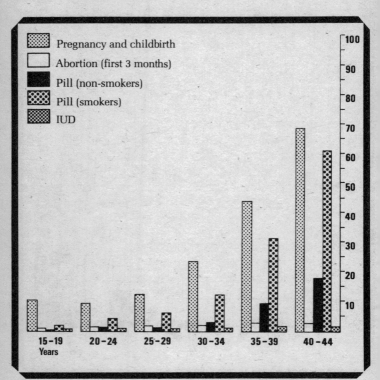

Legend:
- Pregnancy and childbirth
- Abortion (first 3 months)
- Pill (non-smokers)
- Pill (smokers)
- IUD

Age groups: 15–19 Years, 20–24, 25–29, 30–34, 35–39, 40–44

Scale: 10, 20, 30, 40, 50, 60, 70, 80, 90, 100

**Risks**
Unfortunately the two most effective reversible forms of contraception — the pill and the IUD — do involve some risk to health. At all ages, however, the mortality risk is less great than that involved in pregnancy and childbirth. This diagram, based on research in the USA by C. Tietze et al (1979), compares deaths in different age groups per 100,000 users of the pill (subdivided into smokers and non-smokers) and the IUD, with those from pregnancy and childbirth (per 100,000 live births) and legal abortion (per 100,000 first trimester abortions).

## Contraceptive situations

Choice of a contraceptive method depends very much on a couple's situation at the time. There are three main contraceptive situations.

**A** Teenagers or young adults at the start of sexual activity often use withdrawal or condoms. Once sexual activity is established, most young women use the pill, which is highly effective and has fewer health risks for the young.

**B** Between children, some women continue with the pill. Others, worried about increased health risks if the pill is used for many years or as they get older, change to the slightly less effective IUD or to a cap.

**C** Once the family is complete, the ideal method of contraception for most couples is probably sterilization of either the man or the woman.

©DIAGRAM

157

# The pill 1

Oral contraception, or the birth pill, is the most reliable reversible method of birth control to date. Since their development in the 1950s, and despite periods of adverse publicity, oral contraceptives have had an enormous success. It has been estimated that in 1966 about 10 million women around the world were "on the pill": by 1977 the figure was about 54 million.

Oral contraceptives contain synthetic versions of the natural female hormones estrogen and progesterone. These hormones are involved in the normal monthly cycle of ovulation and menstruation. By altering the natural hormone balance of a woman's body, oral contraceptives interfere with this cycle and suppress fertility.

There are many different brands of pill available, but there are two basic types: the combined pill, containing both estrogen and progestogen (synthetic progesterone), and the minipill, which contains only progestogen. The combined pill works mainly by suppressing ovulation. The minipill does not always suppress ovulation, its main effects being on the cervical mucus and the uterus lining.

The pill must be prescribed by a doctor. Used properly it is highly effective. It is also easy to use and does not interfere with lovemaking. The combined pill ensures regular

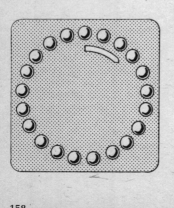

**Taking the combined pill**
This usually comes in packs of 21, each pack being taken on a monthly basis. Unless the doctor gives other instructions, the first pack of pills is started on day 5 of a period whether bleeding has stopped or not. Thereafter one pill is taken each day until the pack is finished. There is a gap of seven pill-free days during which bleeding occurs. A new pack is then started.

menstruation, and may help to relieve premenstrual tension and menstrual pain.

Most women on the pill feel quite healthy, but side effects are fairly common. These include nausea, sore breasts, headaches, tiredness or weight gain. Usually most disappear within the first two or three months; if not, a change of pill may be recommended. Some women experience depression or intensified mood changes, and in severe cases a doctor may suggest stopping the pill.

A great deal has been written about the dangers of oral contraception. Research has shown that the pill, particularly high-estrogen brands, makes the blood clot more easily and can lead to thrombosis. This risk cannot be denied, but it is fairly small and is most applicable to women who smoke, have raised blood pressure, are diabetic, or whose relatives have had heart attacks. As the risk increases with age, women over 35 are usually advised not to take the combined pill. It is thought that the minipill may be less dangerous for older women, but long-term effects are not yet known.

To regain fertility, a woman needs only to stop taking the pill. Sometimes ovulation resumes at once, in other women it may take several months: 98% of all women on the pill ovulate within three months of stopping taking it.

### Taking the minipill
This comes in packs of 28 pills. The first pill of the first course is taken on day 1 of a period. Thereafter one pill is taken every day, even during menstruation. The minipill must be taken at the same time every day.

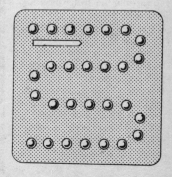

©DIAGRAM

# The pill 2

**Normal and pill-affected cycles**
Here we compare hormone levels
(**a**) in the normal monthly cycle
and in the cycles of pill-users,
and show how these affect
ovulation (**b**), the cervical mucus
(**c**) and the uterus lining (**d**).

**1 Normal menstrual cycle**
After menstruation, low estrogen
levels stimulate production of
FSH and LH, which cause an egg
follicle to mature, estrogen to be
released by the follicle, and
ovulation to occur. The follicle
then produces estrogen and
progesterone, causing the uterus
lining to build up. If no egg is
fertilized, these hormone levels
drop and menstruation (**e**) occurs.

**When starting the pill,** a second
contraceptive is needed for the
first 14 days (except when the
doctor gives instructions to
start taking the pill on day 1).
**Diarrhea or vomiting** may stop
the pill from being absorbed, so
use a second contraceptive
during the illness and for 14 days
after it.
**Drugs,** including some sedatives,
pain-killers and antibiotics,
interfere with the pill's action;
check with the doctor if taking
any medication.
**If you forget** to take one pill, take
it as soon as possible, ideally
within 12 hours of the usual time,
even if this means taking two
pills on one day.
If you forget two pills, finish the
pack normally but use a second
contraceptive for 14 days.
**Unusual bleeding** or "spotting"
is rarely important, but always
inform the doctor.

**2 Combined pill cycle**
High levels of estrogen and
progestogen are maintained for
about three out of four weeks.
This suppresses production of
the pituitary hormones FSH and
LH. Consequently ovulation does
not occur, the cervical mucus is
thick and impenetrable to sperm
throughout the cycle, and the
uterus lining does not build up
enough to support an embryo.

**3 Minipill cycle**
These progestogen-only pills
maintain an intermediate level of
progestogen throughout the
cycle. Estrogen is produced
naturally, but the peaks are
lower. Ovulation is not always
prevented. This pill mainly
works by thickening the cervical
mucus and making it
impenetrable to sperm. The
uterus lining is also affected.

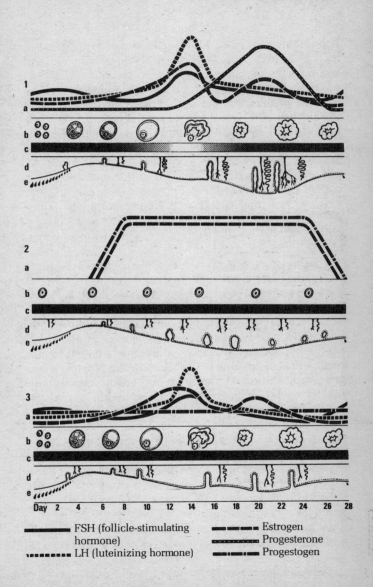

1

2

3

Day 2 4 6 8 10 12 14 16 18 20 22 24 26 28

—————— FSH (follicle-stimulating
hormone)

■ ■ ■ ■ ■ LH (luteinizing hormone)

■ ■ ■ ■ Estrogen

.............. Progesterone

■ ▪ ■ ▪ ■ Progestogen

# The IUD 1

An intrauterine device (also known as an IUD, IUCD, coil or loop) is a small, flexible device, inserted by a doctor into a woman's uterus where it acts as a contraceptive. The idea is not new; it is said that in biblical times camel drivers inserted pebbles into the uteri of camels to prevent them from conceiving, and the first twentieth century IUD to be inserted into a woman was used as long ago as 1909. Modern IUDs came into being during the 1950s and 1960s, at about the same time as the pill. They are made of polyethylene plastic, sometimes wound around with copper or impregnated with progesterone, and usually have a nylon "tail" that extends from the cervix into the vagina. IUDs were originally restricted to women who had had children; today smaller designs mean that women without children can also use them.

An IUD is effective as soon as it is fitted, and can remain in the uterus for one, two or more years according to type. Tampons can still be used. An IUD has no effect on lovemaking, and is nearly as efficient as the pill. But just how it works is still a matter of controversy. It is thought that local foreign body inflammation or increased local production of hormones may inhibit implantation, or that mechanical dislodging of the blastocyst (p. 123) may occur after implantation. The addition of copper to various types of IUD seems to increase the contraceptive effect. To regain fertility a woman need only have the IUD removed.

There are a number of possible side effects. The most common are heavy periods and pain, and about 15-20% of users have their IUDs removed as a result. Pelvic infection, though less common, is more likely to occur in IUD users, especially among younger women with multiple partners. If left untreated, pelvic infection can be extremely dangerous, causing infertility and even death. A doctor must be told about any past infections before fitting an IUD, and should be informed at once of any symptoms such as ill-smelling vaginal discharge or abdominal pain accompanied by fever. A further, very rare problem is perforation of the uterus. More common is the problem of expulsion; the IUD falls out, perhaps unnoticed. Risk of expulsion is greatest in the first three months after fitting and in young women who have not had children. Expulsion is uncommon after the first year. If pregnancy occurs with an IUD in position, the IUD should be removed, as its presence increases the risk of miscarriage and infection.

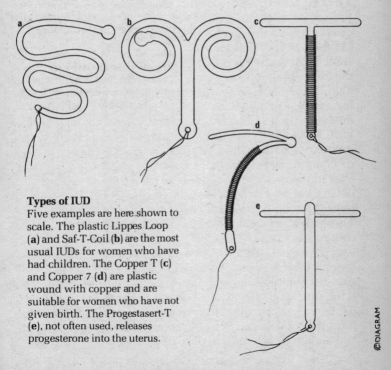

**Types of IUD**
Five examples are here shown to scale. The plastic Lippes Loop (**a**) and Saf-T-Coil (**b**) are the most usual IUDs for women who have had children. The Copper T (**c**) and Copper 7 (**d**) are plastic wound with copper and are suitable for women who have not given birth. The Progestasert-T (**e**), not often used, releases progesterone into the uterus.

©DIAGRAM

# The IUD 2

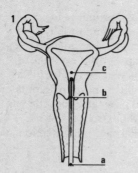

### Insertion

An IUD must be fitted by a doctor or other trained person, ideally during a period or immediately afterwards. The process takes only a few minutes. For insertion, IUDs are elongated in a double-barreled plastic inserter.

**1** The inserter (**a**) is passed through the cervical os (**b**) into the uterus (**c**).

**2** The IUD is propelled out into the uterus, where it assumes its normal shape (**d**). The inserter is then removed, and the plastic tail threads of the IUD cut to their desired length.

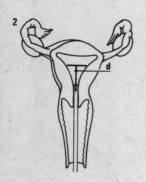

### After effects

Pain after insertion typically lasts 24-48 hours. Increased cramps tend to occur with the next few periods, and bleeding is usually heavier.

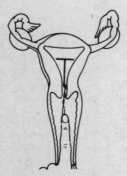

### Checking

The IUD's tail threads hang down from the cervix into the vagina. As a result a woman can — and should — learn to feel for these threads with her finger. She can then make regular checks to ensure that the IUD is still in place. If the threads cannot be felt, extra contraception should be used and a doctor must be consulted as soon as possible.

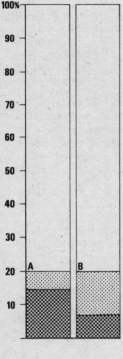

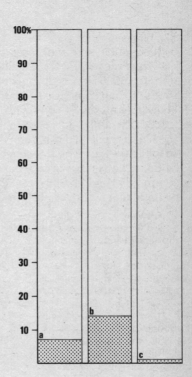

**Bleeding problems**
An estimated 15-20% (**A**) of users have their IUDs removed because of heavy bleeding and increased pain at menstruation. Most IUDs increase menstrual bleeding, but the Progestasert-T reduces it.

**Expulsion**
Expulsion is most likely in the first few months. Expulsion rates for the first year are estimated at between 7% and 20% (**B**).

**Infection**
The risk of pelvic infection — pelvic inflammatory disease, or PID — is increased in IUD users. A survey by London's Margaret Pyke Centre showed that of 871 women (none who had had children) fitted with IUDs in 1975-76, a total (**a**) of 7% suffered from PID. For those aged 16-19 years (**b**) the figure was 14%; for ages 30-49 (**c**) it was only 1.2%.

©DIAGRAM

# Caps and spermicides 1

The cap is used by only about 6% of all women who use contraception, and until recently has been regarded by many people as "old fashioned" and even distasteful. But until the 1960s it was the only reasonably reliable method that a woman could use to control her own fertility. Above all a cap is absolutely safe, causing no side effects at all. For this reason, and as a reaction to the side effects of the pill and the IUD, more and more women are again showing interest in using the cap, which is suitable for women of all ages. Of the various types of cap, the diaphragm is the most commonly used. But other smaller caps are sometimes recommended; the cervical cap, for example, is especially

**Types of cap**
Four different types of cap are illustrated here.
**a** The diaphragm is the largest type of cap, and is the most commonly used. It consists of a soft rubber dome mounted on a pliable metal rim.
**b** The cervical cap is a smaller thimble-shaped cap. Most are rubber with a raised hollow rim.
**c** The vault cap is a bowl-shaped cap with a thin center and a thicker rim. It is held in position by suction when the center is depressed.
**d** The vimule cap combines features of the cervical and the vault cap. It is dome-shaped with a flanged rim that holds it in position by suction.

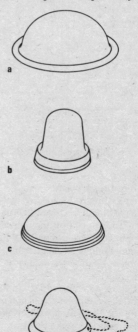

suitable for women with weak pelvic floor muscles. Once in place, the cap acts as a "barrier" to sperm. Used carefully, always with a spermicide, it is extremely effective; one study, at the Margaret Sanger Research Bureau, New York in 1976, showed an effectiveness rate of 98%.
The cap must be fitted by a trained person, and then checked at regular intervals. Instructions on insertion and on the use of spermicides are given at the time of fitting. Basically, spermicide is applied to the cap before insertion and then more spermicide may be put into the vagina. The cap must be left in position for at least 6 hours after intercourse. If intercourse is delayed more than 2 hours, extra spermicide

**Caps in position**
Here we show three types of cap in position in the vagina.
**A** The diaphragm fits across the vaginal vault, shielding the cervix during intercourse by fitting closely into the upper vaginal walls.
**B** The cervical cap fits closely around the base of the cervix.
**C** The vault cap clings to the vaginal vault by suction.

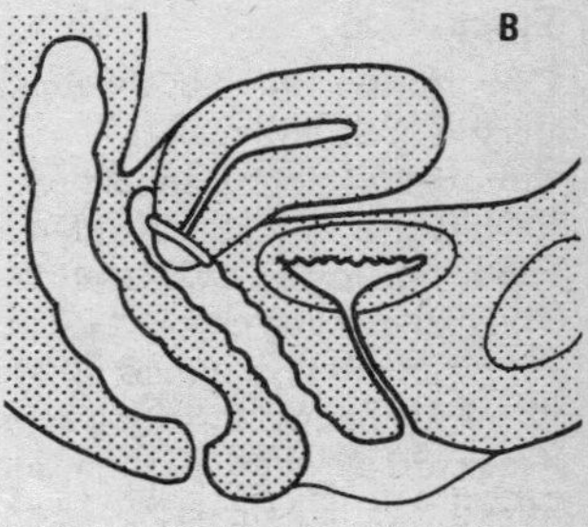


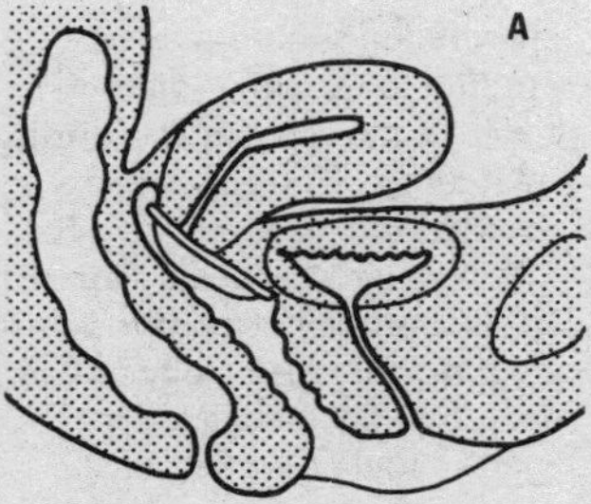


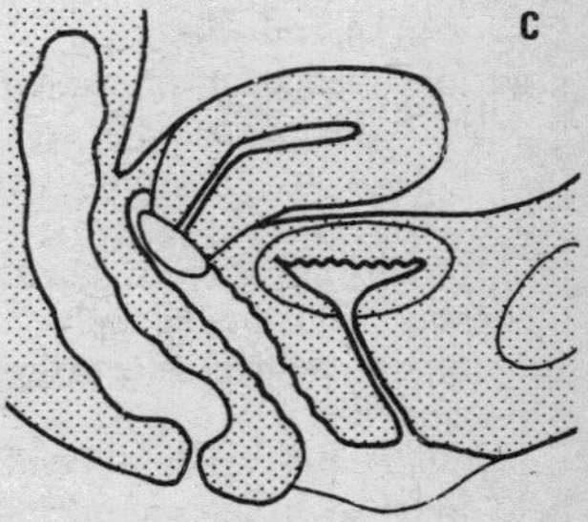

# Caps and spermicides 2

should be used. If intercourse is repeated, the cap must on no account be taken out but additional spermicide should be put into the vagina.

After use, the cap should be washed gently with warm water and unperfumed soap, rinsed, dried, and stored in a cool place. Check it regularly for holes and tears.

**Spermicides** are chemical products that either destroy sperm or create a barrier of foam or fluid. They come in various forms including creams, jellies, aerosol foams and pessaries. Inadequate if used alone, they greatly increase the effectiveness of a cap or condom.

### Fitting

Caps must be fitted by a trained person, who will make a thorough vaginal examination. Each type is available in different sizes, and correct fit is essential. The cap must be checked for fit every six months. It must also be checked after the birth of a baby, a miscarriage or an abortion, and after a weight gain or loss of more than 7lb (3kg).

### Caps and spermicides

Caps give inadequate protection unless used with spermicides. Individual instructions are given when a cap is fitted; we give the basic procedures of one method. It is essential always to apply spermicidal cream or jelly to the cap before it is inserted. As shown here, the cap should be held dome down and spermicide squeezed into it. A thin film of spermicide should then be applied to the rim — not too much or the cap may slip during intercourse. The cap is then inserted into the vagina, to be followed by more spermicide. An applicator may be used to squirt spermicidal cream, jelly or foam deep into the vagina, or spermicidal pessaries may be used; all instructions must be followed with care.

## Insertion

Inserting a diaphragm is probably easiest if you stand with one foot on a stool or lavatory seat. Hold the edges of the diaphragm together and push it by hand into the vagina (**a**). Push the diaphragm against the back wall of the vagina as far as possible so that it passes behind the cervix (**b**). The diaphragm will then spring back into its normal shape so that it is held in place over the cervix. Check the diaphragm with a finger to ensure that it is fully covering the cervix (**c**).

When the cap is correctly in place it will not interfere with lovemaking and neither partner should be able to feel it.

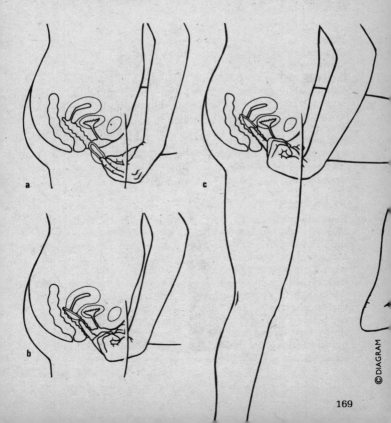

# Rhythm method 1

The rhythm method — also known as the "safe period," "natural birth control" or "fertility awareness" — is the only method of birth control allowed by the Roman Catholic Church and as a result is used by a fairly large number of people. It is based on an understanding of a woman's natural monthly cycle and involves only having sexual intercourse during the least fertile (or "safe") periods of the month. This means that sexual intercourse must be avoided around the time of ovulation, when an egg is released for fertilization and the likelihood of pregnancy is greatest. The main problem is to establish when ovulation occurs, as there is no

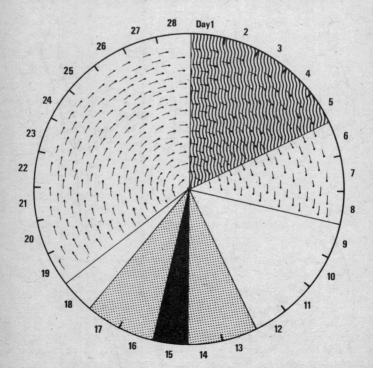

obvious sign and very few women have a regular 28-day cycle. There are three main rhythm techniques, which are often used in combination.

**Calendar method** This method is based on studying the length of previous menstrual cycles in order to calculate when ovulation is likely in the present cycle. Details for calculating this information and also the times when intercourse is or is not safe are given in the captions to our diagrams. Women with irregular menstrual cycles are warned not to rely solely on the calendar method, but may like to combine it with another rhythm technique.

**Calendar method (28-day cycle)**
All rhythm methods are based on avoiding sexual intercourse around the time of ovulation, when an egg is available for fertilization. For women with a regular 28-day cycle the basic calendar method allows this "unsafe" period to be ascertained with reasonable accuracy. (Only about 8% of women, however, have such a cycle.) In theory, ovulation takes place 14 days before the next menstruation (ie day 15 of the cycle). In practice, however, it can occur anywhere from day 13 to day 17. Sperm can survive within the woman for 72 hours or more, so four more days should be added before the likely time of ovulation (ie starting on day 9). After ovulation an egg is available for fertilization for 24 hours, so a further unsafe day must be added after the last likely time of ovulation (day 18). Thus 10 days (9 to 18) are unsafe.

**Key**
Safe days
Unsafe days
Menstruation (safe)
Ovulation likely (unsafe)
Ovulation (unsafe)

©DIAGRAM

# Rhythm method 2

**Temperature method** A woman's resting or basal body temperature rises by as much as 1°F (0.6°C) in the days after ovulation. By taking her temperature daily, preferably with a rectal or a special BBT thermometer, a woman can identify the safe period after ovulation (see caption to diagram). This method does not identify a safe period before ovulation.

**Mucus method** This method involves learning to recognize variations in the quantity and character of cervical mucus at different times in the monthly cycle (see caption). Some women merely use finger examination of the vagina, others use a speculum to inspect the cervix.

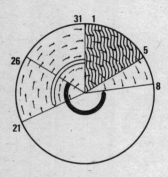

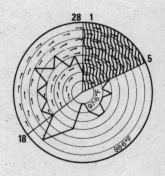

**Calendar method (irregular)**
Using records based on their last 12 cycles, women with irregular periods can use this formula to calculate their unsafe days. The first unsafe day is found by taking 18 from the number of days in their shortest cycle (in our example, 26−18 = day 8). The last unsafe day is found by taking 10 from the length of the longest cycle (eg, 31-10 = day 21).

**Temperature method**
The diagram shows variations in a woman's basal body temperature during the monthly cycle. The temperature rises just after ovulation and then stays higher until the next period. The temperature is taken each day at the same time, ideally in the morning before getting out of bed. Intercourse becomes safe three days after the rise begins.

**Advantages and disadvantages** The main advantages of the rhythm method are that it is completely natural and has no physical side effects. Even the problem of sexual frustration can be overcome by incorporating techniques other than intercourse into lovemaking. But the rhythm method is unreliable and to be effective usually needs skilled counseling, experience and self-discipline. More seriously, there is some evidence that method failure may increase the risk of fetal abnormality as conception is liable to occur when either the ovum or the sperm are reaching the end of their "life span."

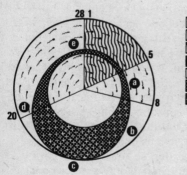

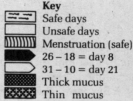

**Key**
Safe days
Unsafe days
Menstruation (safe)
26 – 18 = day 8
31 – 10 = day 21
Thick mucus
Thin mucus

**Mucus method**
The diagram shows monthly changes in cervical secretions:
**a** moderate amount, thick, cloudy;
**b** increasing amount, thick to thin, mixed cloudy and clear;
**c** maximum amount, very thin and slippery, clear;
**d** decreasing amount, thin, mixed cloudy and clear;
**e** tiny amount, thick, cloudy.

© DIAGRAM

# Male methods 1

There are two traditional male methods of contraception: coitus interruptus and the condom. Both have been known for thousands of years and both are still extremely popular; worldwide they are more commonly used than the pill or the IUD. Neither coitus interruptus nor the condom needs any medical supervision, and there are no physical side effects. But their success does depend on a man being prepared to accept full responsibility and to exercise control and consideration.

**Coitus interruptus,** also known as "withdrawal" or "being careful," is the oldest and simplest method of birth control in existence. The male partner takes his penis out of the woman's vagina (withdraws) just before orgasm, and as a result semen is ejaculated outside her body and away from her vagina. For some couples this method works well but in general it is very unreliable. Failure may occur because some fluid containing sperm "weeps" from the penis before orgasm or because the man fails to withdraw properly. And even if the penis is withdrawn from the vagina, if any semen is ejaculated onto the vulva or surrounding skin sperm can still swim into the vagina. Continued use of withdrawal can also be frustrating and lead to tension.

**The condom,** also known as the "sheath," "rubber," or "French letter," is much more reliable. A condom consists of a thin rubber sheath open at one end and closed at the other. It fits tightly over the man's erect penis so that when he ejaculates the semen is trapped inside the sheath. Used carefully, and ideally with a spermicide, condoms are an excellent form of birth control. They are easy to obtain, carry around and use, and they are the only contraceptive that offers protection against some types of venereal disease. Failure tends to occur because condoms are used inconsistently or because a couple, not wishing to interrupt the spontaneity of lovemaking, decide to "take a risk."

# Birth control

## Types of condom

All condoms are a standard 7in (18cm) size but they do come in a variety of types including plain-ended (**a**) or teat-ended (**b,c**). They may also be colored (**d**), textured (**e**) or lubricated. Lubricated brands are claimed to increase penile sensitivity. Condoms are sold in sealed packets and, kept from heat, have a shelf life of up to 2 years.

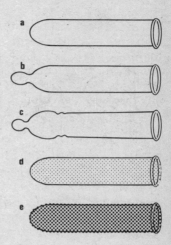

## Arguments for and against

Listed in the box are some of the arguments commonly made for and against condoms. During the 1960s and 1970s condoms lost popularity in favor of the pill and IUD, but worries about the physical effects of these methods are causing some couples to overcome old prejudices against the condom.

### Arguments for condoms

**1** Widely available from stores, vending machines and by mail.
**2** Inexpensive.
**3** Easy to carry around.
**4** Reasonably efficient if properly used; better if used with a spermicide.
**5** No physical side effects for either partner.
**6** Protection against some forms of VD.

### Arguments against condoms

**1** Embarrassing to purchase.
**2** Intercourse must be planned and condoms obtained first.
**3** Embarrassing to carry around.
**4** Not as efficient as some other methods of birth control.
**5** Unpleasant associations.
**6** Lack of spontaneity: pause to put the condom on and care needed at withdrawal.
**7** Claimed lack of sensitivity.

© DIAGRAM

# Male methods 2

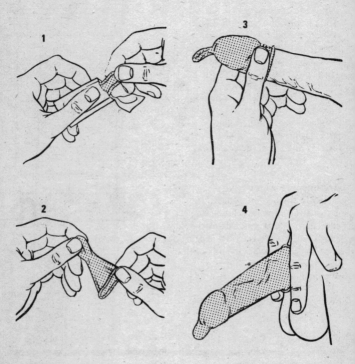

**Using a condom**

1 Carefully remove the rolled condom from its foil packet.

2 Unroll about an inch of the condom and squeeze the tip between the thumb and forefinger to leave an empty space beyond the penis to catch the sperm and prevent the condom bursting.

3 Unroll the condom onto the erect penis; either partner can do this and the action can be incorporated into lovemaking. Be careful not to damage the condom with your fingernails. Do not use Vaseline or other grease as a lubricant.

4 After orgasm and before his erection subsides the man must withdraw his penis from his partner's vagina, taking care to hold the rim of the condom close to his penis as he does so.

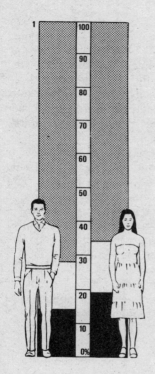

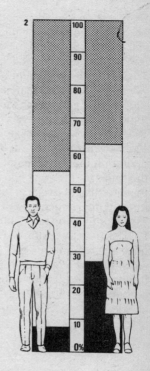

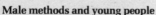

**Male methods and young people**

A survey conducted in the UK in 1974-75 showed male methods of contraception to be very popular among sample groups of young people aged 16-19 years (taken from *My Mother Said* by Christine Farrell, published by Routledge & Kegan Paul).

**Key**
- ▨ Sheath
- ☐ Withdrawal
- ■ Others

**1** Method used on first occasion and always thereafter:
sheath: 72% men, 66% women;
withdrawal: 14% men, 15% women;
others: 14% men, 19% women.

**2** No method used on first occasion, but used later:
sheath: 46% men, 38% women;
withdrawal: 47% men, 35% women;
others: 7% men, 27% women.

©DIAGRAM

# Sterilization 1

Sterilization is an ideal method of contraception for couples who want no further children. It is a highly effective, once and for all solution to the problem of birth control. Contrary to popular prejudice, it does not interfere with the sex drive, virility or the enjoyment of sex. In fact many men and women report that their enjoyment of sex is increased once the fear of pregnancy is so absolutely removed. The decision to be sterilized, however, requires careful thought, for the chances of reversal are generally not very good.

**Male sterilization,** or vasectomy, is a minor surgical operation that involves cutting and tying the vas deferens, the tubes that carry sperm from the testes to the penis. The man continues to ejaculate as normal but the semen no longer carries sperm, which are reabsorbed by the body. Vasectomy is the safest surgical method of birth control so far. It is usually performed in an outpatient clinic, and takes only a few minutes. Pain, swelling and bruising soon subside, and most men can return to work after 2 days. Intercourse can be resumed after a week, but a second contraceptive must be used, sometimes for 3-4 months, until checks show that the semen is completely free of sperm.

**Vasectomy**
Under a local anesthetic and through a small incision in the scrotum each vas deferens is isolated and a small piece, about ½in long, cut out. The cut ends are then folded back and tied. The scrotal incisions are then stitched.

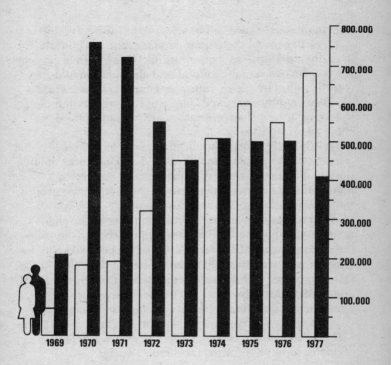

**Popularity of sterilization**
During the 1970s improvements in sterilization techniques and the removal of various legal and cultural barriers meant that male and female sterilization greatly increased in popularity. Our diagram shows estimates of male and female sterilizations in the USA between 1969 and 1977. In this period roughly 4.6 million men and 3.6 million women were sterilized in the USA. Although male sterilizations far outnumbered female sterilizations in the early part of this period, female sterilization is now the more popular operation.

© DIAGRAM

# Sterilization 2

**Female sterilization** can be achieved in a variety of different ways. In general, operations involve cutting or blocking the Fallopian tubes, so preventing the eggs' normal journey from the ovaries to the uterus and also their possible fertilization by sperm. (Surgical removal of the uterus, Fallopian tubes or ovaries also result in sterility but these actions are considered unnecessarily drastic to be done purely to sterilize.)

Traditionally, female sterilization has been by tubal ligation, an operation in which the Fallopian tubes are tied and cut. Alternatively, the tubes may be blocked by cauterization. Newer developments include the use of clips, elastic rings and other blocking devices.

The traditional operation, involving major abdominal surgery, requires a hospital stay of 5-6 days and a typical recovery period of 6 weeks. A revolution occurred with the development of so-called laparoscopic sterilizations, in which surgery is reduced to a minimum. Both the standard laparoscopic sterilization and the newer minilaparotomy may be performed under local anesthetic in an outpatient department, although a general anesthetic involving a 1 or 2 days' hospital stay is often preferred. Recovery after a laparoscopic sterilization takes only 2-6 days.

## Female sterilization

**1** The female reproductive tract is here shown after a tubal ligation. The traditional operation, requiring a general anesthetic, is performed through a 2-3in incision in the abdomen. Alternatively, entry may be by way of the vagina. A section of each tube is pulled up, tied and then cut; the cut ends heal with a gap between them.

**2** This diagram shows a one-entry laparoscopic sterilization. It is done under either a general or a local anesthetic. A tiny incision is made in the area of the navel, through which the surgeon inserts an instrument comprising a laparoscope (**a**), which allows him to see into the abdominal cavity, and cauterizing forceps (**b**), which he uses to block the tubes.

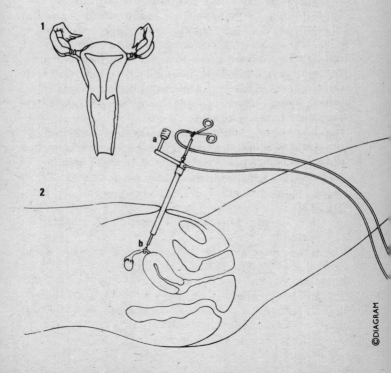

# Postcoital methods

Effective postcoital or "after the event" methods of contraception have now been available for some time, but their use remains fairly limited. In general the chances of conceiving after one act of unprotected intercourse around the time of ovulation are estimated at between 2% and 20%. Before the development of postcoital contraceptives a couple faced with this possibility of pregnancy could do no more than sit and hope that the woman's period would begin. Today a woman who thinks she may be pregnant has no need to wait until pregnancy can be confirmed. There are three different methods of postcoital contraception currently available — the "morning after pill," the "morning after IUD," and menstrual extraction.

The morning after pill consists of very large doses of a synthetic estrogen, which must be started within 72 hours of unprotected intercourse and continued over a five-day period. As yet, the morning after pill must be seen only as an emergency measure; side effects can be very severe and there is considerable risk of damage to the fetus if pregnancy is not prevented.

The morning after IUD is a standard Copper 7 inserted within the first few days after unprotected intercourse. It is a highly effective postcoital contraceptive that works by setting up an inflammatory reaction that interferes with implantation. Side effects are not usually severe, and the IUD can be left in position as a normal contraceptive. Risk of infection makes postcoital IUD insertion unsuitable for rape victims.

Menstrual extraction, also known as menstrual regulation, can be performed up to two weeks after a period was due. It consists of using suction to extract the uterus lining and also any fetal tissue that may be present. The procedure usually takes no more than 10 minutes, and the woman can leave unaided within a half hour.

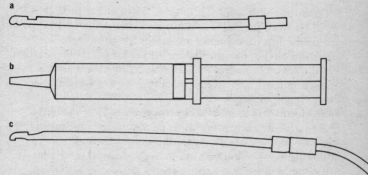

## Menstrual extraction equipment

The uterus lining is extracted through a small, hollow, flexible plastic cannula (**a**). This is attached either to a specially designed syringe (**b**) or, by means of a hose (**c**), to an electrically powered suction machine.

## Extraction procedure

The doctor inserts a speculum (**1**) and washes the cervix with antiseptic. The cervix is held in place with a tenaculum (**2**), and a local anesthetic is then applied. A lubricated 4mm or 6mm cannula (**3**) is next inserted into the uterus. Suction (**4**) is then applied, and the cannula moved around the uterine cavity until all the tissue is removed.

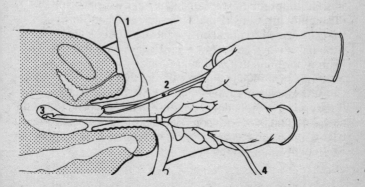

©DIAGRAM

# Research

Although contraception today is fairly sophisticated, it is still far from perfect. For many people the methods already described in this chapter are either too risky, too complicated or too unreliable. While it is unlikely that there will ever be one ideal, risk-free, foolproof method it is possible that the next few decades will see some quite startling changes.

**Developments in female contraceptives** Most current research into contraception is concentrated on improving female methods, with particular emphasis on the development of long-acting, hormone-based methods. An injectable hormonal contraceptive known as Depo-Provera already exists and has been widely used in the Third World. Based on the same principle as the minipill, it is a slow-release progestogen injection given every 3 or 6 months. It is very effective but can cause severe side effects and is not often used in the USA or UK. Progesterone-impregnated IUDs have also been developed, but again are not often used. Other possibilities include intravaginal rings, small time-release hormone capsules, and contraceptive bracelets. Distant possibilities include a hormone nasal spray which, sniffed once a day, would act on the pituitary gland to prevent ovulation, and special infertility vaccines that would immunize a woman against her partner's sperm.

**The male pill** Considerable research also continues on developing a hormonal birth control technique for men, but this has always presented a particular problem — how to find a hormone that will suppress sperm manufacture without suppressing a man's libido. Promising research is taking place in China where a birth pill containing gossypol, a component of cottonseed oil, has been tested on some 10,000 men with considerable success. It is, however, likely to be some years before a satisfactory male pill is widely available in the West.

# Birth control

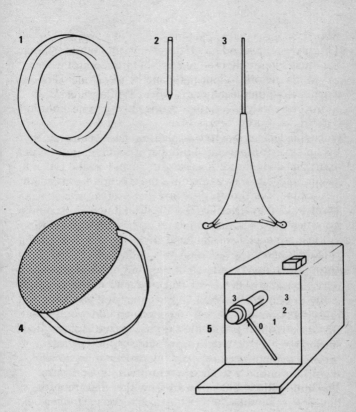

## Some current developments

1 Slow-release progestogen-impregnated intravaginal ring.
2 Small time-release hormone pellets for implantation into a woman's forearm or buttock.
3 Intracervical device designed to release either progestogen or a spermicidal substance.

4 Vaginal sponge impregnated with spermicide; inserted before sex and kept in for 6 hours after.
5 Ovutimer showing mucus changes for the rhythm method

©DIAGRAM

# Abortion 1

Abortion — the deliberate termination of a pregnancy — is a highly emotive and much debated issue. But it remains the most commonly used method of birth control in the world; nearly one in four pregnancies are estimated to be terminated either legally or illegally. While choosing an abortion is rarely easy, it may be the only practical solution. Careful counseling is essential.

Once the decision to have an abortion has been made, time becomes very important. A number of countries now permit abortions up to the 28th week of pregnancy, but it is much easier, safer and less traumatic if the abortion is carried out in the first three months (the first trimester) of pregnancy.

**Dilation and evacuation (D & E),** also known as vacuum curettage, is the most commonly used method of abortion. A local or general anesthetic is given, the cervix is gently dilated (opened), a vacurette or suction curette is passed through the cervix into the uterus, and the fetal material is gently suctioned out. D & E can be carried out up to 12 and sometimes even 16 weeks of pregnancy and is a quick and simple procedure that can be performed under outpatient conditions. Little preparation is needed, the abortion itself takes only about 10 minutes, and recovery time is fast. There is usually some bleeding, possibly with cramps, for about a week; normal periods should return within 4-6 weeks.

**Dilation and curettage (D & C)** is another first-trimester abortion technique, but has now been largely superseded by D & E. The cervix is dilated and the uterine contents are then scraped out with a metal curette. Although D & C is still used, it is more complicated and painful, requires a general anesthetic, and carries greater risks of uterine perforation and infection.

**Late abortions** usually rely on inducing miscarriage. A general anesthetic is given, the amniotic fluid is withdrawn and replaced with either a saline (salt) or prostaglandin (naturally-occurring hormone) solution. The fetus dies and within 6-48 hours the cervix dilates, contractions begin and "labor" occurs. As a result the fetus and placenta are expelled. This type of abortion is quite complicated, carries a number of risks, and is so similar to normal labor that it can be a very distressing experience.

**Hysterotomy** is a very rarely used method of late abortion. In principle it is very similar to a Caesarian birth and involves major surgery. It is the most complicated method of abortion and carries the highest risks.

**Risks: abortion and pregnancy**
The risk of a woman dying as a result of a legal abortion is on average considerably lower than that involved in pregnancy and childbirth. Our diagram, based on US statistics for 1972-76, shows a mortality rate of three per 100,000 legal abortions (**A**), compared to 14.6 maternal deaths during pregnancy and childbirth for every 100,000 live births (**B**).

**Risks: abortion techniques**
Different abortion techniques involve different degrees of risk. This diagram, based on US statistics for 1972-76, shows the mortality rate for every 100,000 abortions performed by each of the following methods.
**a** D&C/D&E 1.7
**b** Amniotic fluid exchange 15.5
**c** Hysterotomy/hysterectomy 42.4
**d** Other 9.9

©DIAGRAM

# Abortion 2

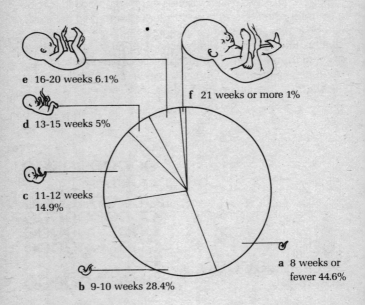

**e** 16-20 weeks 6.1%

**d** 13-15 weeks 5%

**c** 11-12 weeks 14.9%

**f** 21 weeks or more 1%

**a** 8 weeks or fewer 44.6%

**b** 9-10 weeks 28.4%

## Timing of abortions

Abortions performed in the USA in 1975 are here broken down according to the duration of pregnancy.

The question of late abortion is hotly debated particularly on ethical grounds. In practice, however, the vast majority of abortions take place in the first three months of pregnancy. Very few women actively seek late abortions, which tend to become necessary either because of delays in confirming pregnancy or in obtaining a legal abortion or because some types of fetal abnormality cannot be detected earlier than 16 weeks.

# Birth control

A Danger to mother's health
B Danger of birth defect in baby
C Family cannot afford the child
D Couple wants no more children

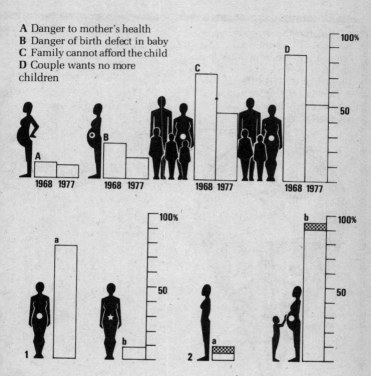

**Attitudes** (*top*)
Surveys in the USA in 1968 and 1977 show increasing acceptance of abortion as a valid method of birth control. The diagram shows the percentage of respondents who disapproved of various grounds for abortion. From 1968 to 1977 the percentage who disapproved of abortion if a couple merely did not want more children fell from 85% to 51%.

**Guilt** (*above*)
Contrary to common fears, it seems that very few women suffer emotionally after an abortion. A New York study (**1**) showed 78% were happy with their decision (**a**); only 8.5% expressed negative feelings or self anger (**b**). But few women repeat the experience (**2**): an estimated 5-10% subsequently have an abortion or illegitimate birth (**a**); 90-95% do not (**b**).

©DIAGRAM

189

# Chapter 8

1 Miniature human curled up in the head of a sperm — an erroneous idea here depicted in an illustration from *Essay de Dioptrique* (1694) by Hartsoeker.
2 Drawing of a highly magnified human ovum, from a medical textbook dated 1907.

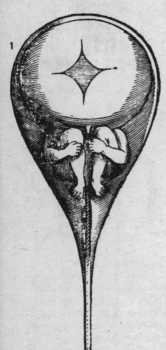

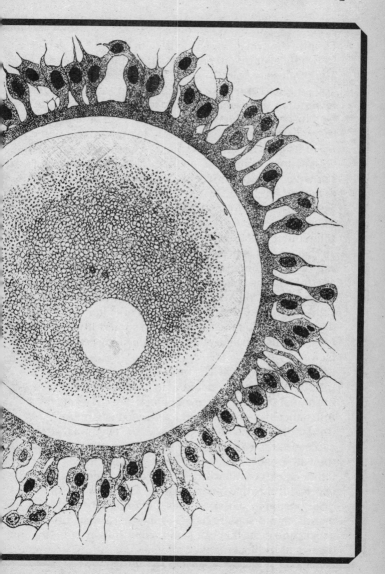

# Causes of infertility 1

Despite the apparent ease with which most couples seem to produce an infant, research shows that one-quarter of all couples are below normal fertility. Ten out of every 100 couples cannot have children, and a further 15 have fewer than they want. Inability to produce children may be a disorder of the woman or of the man or of both. In many cases the condition is only temporary and will clear up of its own accord or respond to medical treatment or counseling. Temporary inability to produce children is known as infertility; where the condition is permanent it is termed sterility.

Successful conception is harder than might at first be imagined. It occurs only when conditions are favorable. Intercourse has to take place around the time of ovulation so that an egg is present for fertilization. The woman's reproductive organs must be healthy and receptive to sperm, and the sperm also must be healthy and fertile. Moreover, once the egg is fertilized, conditions must be right for it to implant itself in the uterus lining for fetal development to proceed. A couple's infertility may result from the disturbance of one or more of these various factors.

**Infertility in women** The most common reason for infertility in women is failure to ovulate, due either to hormonal disorders or to emotional stress. Hormonal imbalance can also prevent a fertilized egg from implanting in the uterus lining, while emotional stress can cause the Fallopian tubes to go into spasm so that they are unable to transport the egg to the uterus.

Other causes of infertility in women include vaginal and cervical fluids that are inadequate for sperm transport or even hostile to sperm, various malformations of the sex organs, and disorders such as venereal disease, fibroids, cancer and cysts that can lead to infertility by affecting the ovaries or by blocking the Fallopian tubes.

**Infertility in men** There are two basic kinds of infertility in men — failure to ejaculate, termed impotence, and infertility of the semen. It may be that the man does not produce enough sperm, or that he produces too much or too little seminal fluid. Too little fluid means that the sperm are not protected against the acidity of the vaginal fluids; too much means that the semen will spill out of the vagina. In some cases the sperm themselves are malformed, or their life span after ejaculation is too short for them to travel far enough to reach the egg.

There are various reasons why infertility occurs in men. Ill health, obesity, poor diet, or a sedentary or stressful life style can all lead to poor sperm production, as can overtight underwear which produces excessive heat around the testicles. Prolonged abstinence from intercourse can also lead to poor sperm production. Other causes of male infertility include failure of the testes to descend before puberty, some childhood illnesses such as mumps that can lead to infertility if contracted as an adult, and various environmental hazards such as exposure to radiation.

**Causes of female infertility**
Some of the common disorders that can affect the female sex organs and cause infertility are:
1 fused labia;
2 a hymen too strong for penetration;
3 a narrow or divided vagina;
4 hostile cervical fluid;
5 a tilted or divided uterus;
6 blocked Fallopian tubes;
7 malfunctioning ovaries.

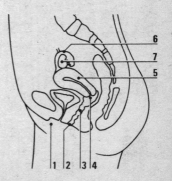

©DIAGRAM

# Causes of infertility 2

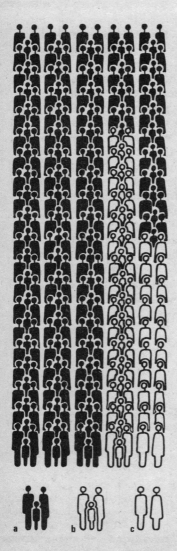

**Incidence of infertility** (*left*)
One-quarter of all couples are below normal fertility. As shown here, out of 100 couples:
**a** 75 can produce as many children as they want;
**b** 15 have fewer children than they want;
**c** 10 cannot have children.

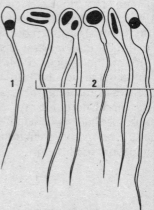

**Abnormal sperm production**
Normal sperm are oval in shape (**1**), but a wide variety of other shapes can also be produced (**2**). On average, male semen contains 10% abnormal sperm, but it can contain as little as 1% or as much as 34%. The higher the percentage of abnormalities, the less likelihood there is of fertility.

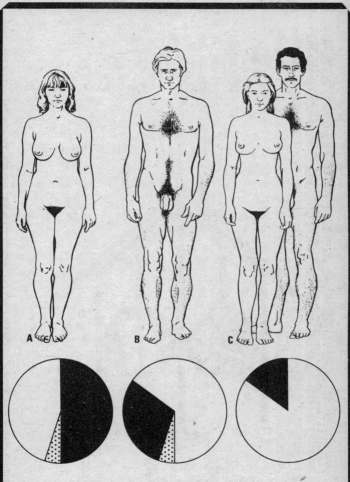

When infertility occurs it may be the woman, the man, or both partners who are infertile. It has been found that in 50-55% of cases it is the woman who is infertile (**A**), in 30-35% of cases it is the man (**B**), and in 15% both are infertile (**C**).

©DIAGRAM

# Tests and advice 1

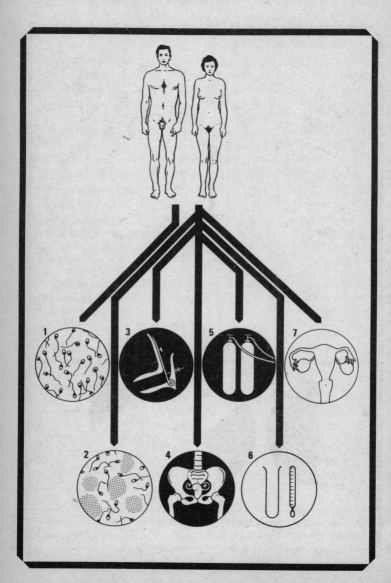

Although the accent today is on reduced family size, prolonged infertility is a very distressing situation for a couple who want children. As a general guideline, if a couple have been having intercourse regularly without contraception for more than a year or so and conception has not occurred, they should seek medical advice. Diagnosis may be quite simple; if not, the couple will be referred to a team of specialists who will carry out a detailed program of investigation on both partners. The source of infertility can then be discovered and in the majority of cases fertility will be restored by treatment.

**Infertility tests**

Specialist infertility tests include the following.

**1** A thorough investigation of the man's semen carried out on a masturbation specimen.

**2** A postcoital test, usually made 6-18 hours after intercourse. This involves examination of mucus taken from the canal of the woman's cervix in order to establish whether the sperm are surviving in the vagina and cervix.

**3** A scrape, or dilation and curettage, in which the lining of the uterus is scraped.

**4** A hystersalpingogram, in which the uterus and Fallopian tubes are X-rayed.

**5** A gas test, or insufflation, in which carbon dioxide is blown through the Fallopian tubes either to clear them or to reveal a blockage.

**6** Tests of ovulation involve daily measuring of progesterone levels in the bloodstream or urine, and daily charting of the body temperature.

**7** A laparoscopy, in which an optical instrument (laparoscope) is inserted into the abdomen so that the ovaries and Fallopian tubes can be examined. This is usually combined with the passage of a colored fluid through the cervix to ascertain whether the tubes are patent (not blocked).

# Tests and advice 2

When cases of infertility are being examined, one of the first questions to be asked is whether the couple are actually having intercourse. Strangely enough, even today, nonconsummation is a frequent cause of infertility. If intercourse is taking place, the questions of timing and of techniques become important. Where a woman has regular 28-day periods, the most fertile phase is usually between days 11 and 16. Where periods are irregular, say cycles of between 27 and 35 days, the chances of conception increase if intercourse takes place on five alternate days starting with the thirteenth day.

**When menstruation is regular**
For women who have a regular 28-day cycle the most fertile period is usually between days 11 and 16, counting from the first day of menstruation.

**When the cycle is irregular**
With an irregular cycle of 27-35 days, conception is more likely if intercourse is on five alternate days, starting on day 13.

Certain positions can also aid fertility, as some positions are more conducive to conception than others. Also fertility in women is always improved if the woman remains fairly still for about a half hour after intercourse. It would also appear that the second half of a man's ejaculate can actually harm sperm, while the first half protects it. Consequently couples are sometimes advised that they can improve the chances of conception if the man withdraws from the woman's vagina halfway through his ejaculation. The couple should then abstain from intercourse for 48 hours.

### Positions for conception

The positions shown increase the chances of conception in the following conditions.

**a** Where obesity is a problem, full or deeper penetration can be achieved if the woman places her knees over the man's shoulders during intercourse.

**b** If vaginal tightness is preventing successful penetration, the vagina can first be dilated by finger or with a glass dilator, and the woman can then squat on top of the man's penis while he lies on his back.

**c** A tilted, or retroverted, uterus is not uncommon in women and usually has no adverse effect on fertility. But where it does, fertility can be helped if the woman lies face-down or kneels and the man enters her from behind.

©DIAGRAM

# Infertility treatments 1

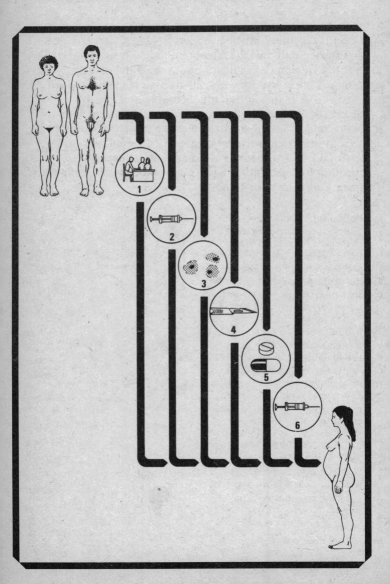

Once the cause of a couple's infertility has been discovered, treatment can take place. Obviously this will vary depending on the problem, but the success rate is fairly high — some clinics claim a 65% success rate within four years of first attendance. The following are some of the treatments that might be recommended.

**Psychiatric help** may be relevant for both partners, as emotional stress and strain can have considerable effects on fertility. Repeated failure to achieve parenthood can itself give rise to mental tension.

**Treating infection** Where infection such as venereal disease is the cause of infertility, the problem can usually be treated with pessaries or with antibiotics.

**Hostility to sperm** If the vaginal or cervical fluids are hostile to sperm, ointments and douches can be used to improve the woman's receptivity. Temporary use of a sheath can sometimes reduce anti-sperm activity.

**Operations** Where a woman's reproductive organs are damaged or malformed there are a number of operations that can be performed quite successfully. Abscesses and cysts can be removed, a rigid hymen can be surgically cut, a narrow vagina can be widened, and a retroverted uterus can be brought forward. Disorders of the cervix, Fallopian tubes and ovaries can also be treated by surgery.

**Treatments for infertility**
An infertile couple now has a very good chance of achieving parenthood, thanks to a wide range of possible management. This includes the following:
1 Psychiatric help
2 Treating infection
3 Overcoming hostility to sperm
4 Operations
5 Fertility drugs
6 Artificial insemination

©DIAGRAM

# Infertility treatments 2

**Fertility drugs** These are sometimes used to boost the fertility of men, but most often they are recommended where tests show that the man is fertile but that the woman's ovaries are not functioning properly although the rest of her reproductive tract is normal. Essentially there are two main drug treatments for women with this type of problem. Clomiphene is usually the first drug to be tried. Exactly how it works is still uncertain, and it was in fact first used as a contraceptive before its reverse effects were discovered. Clomiphene is usually given in a five- to seven-day course during one menstrual cycle. Ovulation should occur within a fortnight. If it does not, the course is repeated up to six times — but no more. This drug has a claimed success rate of 30%, and multiple pregnancies are unlikely since only one ovum is generally released. The second common fertility drug is Pergonal — an extract of FSH and LH hormones obtained from menopausal women. The drug is injected, under close hospital supervision. Ideally only one or two ova will be produced, but this is the drug that has led to most multiple births as well as other serious side effects.

**Artificial insemination** This is the main technique used to overcome male infertility from causes other than emotional stress or poor general health. In artificial insemination sperm are transferred, usually by syringe, onto the woman's cervix on three or four successive days around ovulation. Artificial insemination with the partner's sperm (AIH) may be used when physical or psychological causes interfere with normal intercourse, or when the man's sperm count is low. Artificial insemination with the sperm of an anonymous donor (AID) is more common, and is used when the male partner is sterile, or if he is the carrier of some hereditary disorder. The success rate from AID is about 66% within the first three months.

# Infertility

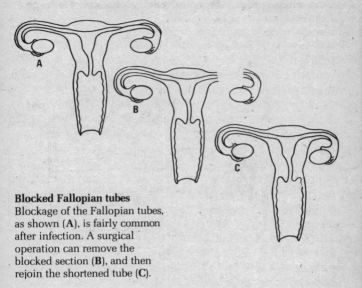

## Blocked Fallopian tubes
Blockage of the Fallopian tubes, as shown (**A**), is fairly common after infection. A surgical operation can remove the blocked section (**B**), and then rejoin the shortened tube (**C**).

## Fertility drugs
Shown here are the cumulative success rates claimed for the two major fertility drugs:
**a** Clomiphene (30%)
**b** Pergonal (15%)

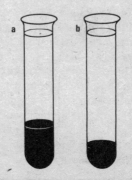

©DIAGRAM

# Chapter 9

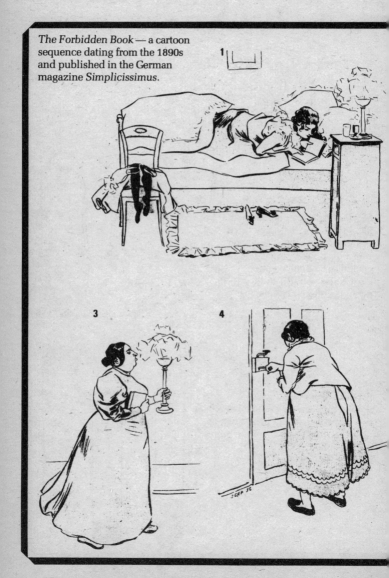

*The Forbidden Book* — a cartoon sequence dating from the 1890s and published in the German magazine *Simplicissimus*.

# Average sexual experience

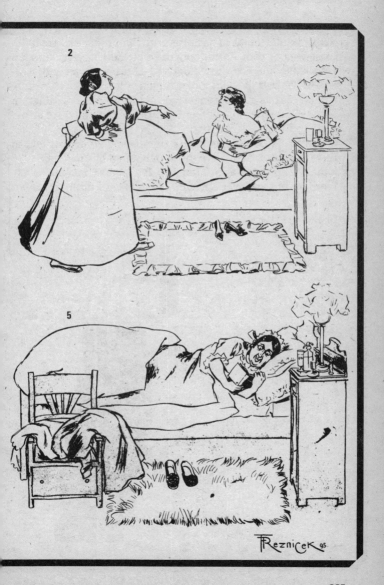

# Early sexual experience 1

This chapter gives facts and figures about general sexual experience from childhood through adolescence and on into adult life. We show how sexual drive varies with age and what part of the population tends to indulge in which sexual outlets at different stages in life. As our first diagram shows, considerable percentages of very young boys and girls indulge in sex play.

Our information comes from a number of surveys. By far the most comprehensive are those published by Alfred C. Kinsey and associates. They involve 12,000 men and 8000 women, but are over 30 years old. Kinsey's findings have

been updated or added to by later studies like Shere Hite's
*The Hite Report* (1976), a nationwide study of American
female sexuality involving 3000 women aged 14 to 78, and
complemented by Antony Pietropinto's and Jacqueline
Simenauer's *Beyond the Male Myth* (1977), based on more
than 4000 American males aged 18 to 65.

Some of the later surveys seem less carefully worded than
Kinsey's: for instance some of Hite's questions were phrased
in ways that evoked unclear answers. But recent studies
undoubtedly reflect the increased freedom of sexual
expression in today's more permissive society.

### Childhood sex play

This diagram shows percentages
of children aged from 5 to 13
engaging in sex play. The
experience of boys is shown to
the left, and of girls to the right
of the center. The figures,
mainly from Kinsey, are largely
based on recollection by adults.
The number of boys who
indulged in sex play increased all
through preadolescence. But the
number of girls fell between ages
9 and 13.

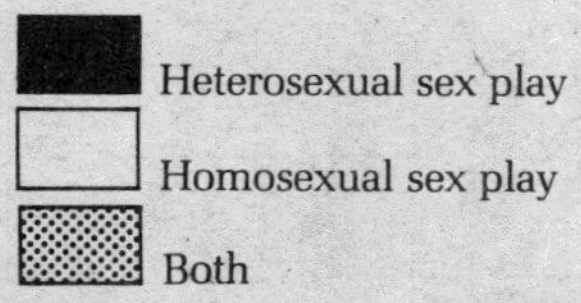

■ Heterosexual sex play

□ Homosexual sex play

▨ Both

©DIAGRAM

# Early sexual experience 2

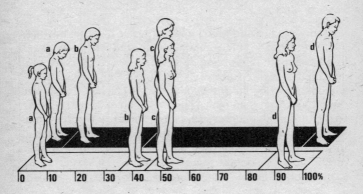

**First masturbation** (*above*)
American teenagers who had masturbated (49% in one survey) were asked when they had started. Here we use research by R.C. Sorensen to show the proportions of males (m) and females (f) who had begun in each of four age groups.

**a** To 10 years: 7% (m), 35% (f).
**b** 11-12 years: 29% (m), 9% (f).
**c** 13-14 years: 55% (m), 40% (f).
**d** 15-19 years: 9% (m), 16% (f).

**Increasing sexual experience** (*below; right*) This series of diagrams is based on a 1971 British survey by H.J. Eysenck of 231 male and 379 female unmarried students aged 18 to 21. Items shown reveal percentages of males and females aged 18 and 21 who had taken part at least once in the activities listed below. Items are broadly arranged in order of probability of experience: people

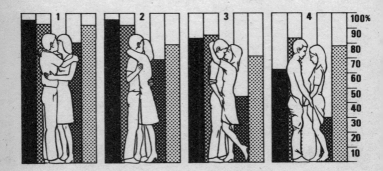

# Average sexual experience

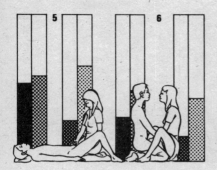

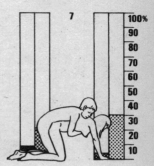

experiencing item **4** have therefore probably experienced items **1**, **2** and **3**.

**1** One minute of continuous lip-to-lip kissing.
**2** Fondling of a woman's breasts over her clothes.
**3** Fondling of a woman's genitals over her clothes.
**4** Manipulation of each other's genitals by man and woman.
**5** Manipulation of male genitals by a woman, to orgasm.

**6** Mutual manipulation of genitals to mutual orgasm.
**7** Sexual intercourse involving a rear-entry position.
**8** Mutual oral manipulation of the partner's genitals.
**9** Mutual oral manipulation of genitals to mutual orgasm.

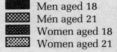

■ Men aged 18
▨ Men aged 21
▦ Women aged 18
▨ Women aged 21

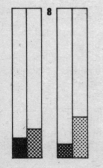

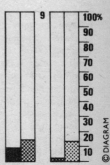

©DIAGRAM

209

# Early sexual experience 3

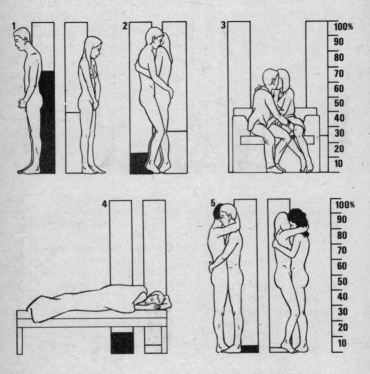

## Sources of first orgasm

These diagrams, using Kinsey's research, compare the five main sources of first orgasm for males and females. Masturbation is seen to be the most common source for both sexes, but for 28% more males than females. More than twice as many males as females first reached orgasm by sex dreams. But twice as many females as males had their first orgasm in intercourse. While nearly a quarter of all women achieved orgasm by petting, fewer than 0.4 men in 100 did so. In both sexes, homosexuality ranked at about the same low level. Rarer first outlets included psychosexual stimuli (1% of women; less than 1% of men).

1 Masturbation 68% (m), 40% (f).
2 Intercourse 13% (m), 27% (f).
3 Petting 0% (m), 24% (f).
4 Sex dreams 13% (m), 5% (f).
5 Homosexuality 4% (m), 3% (f).

# First intercourse 1

Since Kinsey's surveys of the 1940s and 1950s, the main change in early sexual experience has been in coitus before marriage. More young males and females than ever now have premarital intercourse; by 1990 the figure may reach 95 per cent. About 25 per cent of "single" college men and women cohabit. More single males than before have sex with women they love; fewer with prostitutes. Most sexually active single people have one partner or very few partners. Sexually active unmarried females average coitus once every 5-10 weeks. Coitus for single males ranges from once ever to 35 times a week.

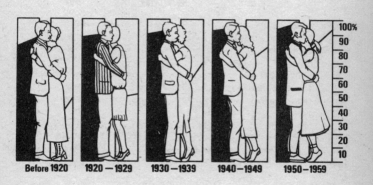

**Before 1920**   **1920 — 1929**   **1930 — 1939**   **1940 — 1949**   **1950 — 1959**

**Sex before marriage**
American men used to be far more sexually active and permissive than American women. Both sexes are now sexually freer than they were, but this is especially true of women. This diagram, based on work by Kinsey, Hunt and Zuckerman, shows percentages of men and women reaching maturity in different decades who had sex before marriage.

©DIAGRAM

211

# First intercourse 2

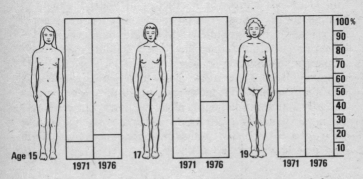

Age 15  1971 1976   17  1971 1976   19  1971 1976   100%  90  80  70  60  50  40  30  20  10

**Teenage sex before marriage** (*above*) Planned Parenthood studies, made in 1971 and 1976, compared for those years the numbers of unmarried girls aged 15 to 19 who had had intercourse. The result reveals an increase of 29% for the group as a whole. The sharpest rise was in those aged 17. In 1976 that age group showed a 54% increase in coitus over the group aged 17 in 1971.

**Age at first intercourse** (*below*) A survey of teenagers published in 1973 (Robert C. Sorensen *Adolescent Sexuality in Contemporary America*) asked if they had ever had intercourse. Our diagram shows percentages who claimed they had.
**a** Boys aged 13-15 years: 44%.
**b** Girls aged 13-15 years: 30%.
**c** Boys aged 16-19 years: 72%.
**d** Girls aged 16-19 years: 57%.

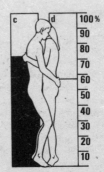

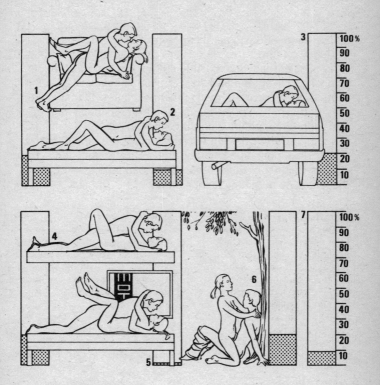

## Place of first intercourse

Sorensen's survey of American teenagers also asked those who were nonvirgins where they had first had intercourse.

Among the boys asked, more had first had sex outdoors than anywhere else, but automobiles ranked first among girls.

None of the boys had first had sex in a hotel bedroom, but 5% of the girls said they had. All of these girls came from the older (16-19) age group. Age also influenced where boys first had sex. Older boys using a car outnumbered younger ones by 3 to 1.

Diagrams show total percentages, given in *Adolescent Sexuality in Contemporary America* (1973).

1 In my home 19%.
2 In a friend's home 10%.
3 In an automobile 20%.
4 In the partner's home 20%.
5 In a hotel or motel 2%.
6 Outdoors 20%.
7 Somewhere else 9%.

© DIAGRAM

# Sexual outlets 1

These pages show general experience of five main sexual outlets based on Kinsey's surveys. At some time in their lives 95% of men and possibly 80% of women masturbate; almost 100% of men and 70% of women have sex dreams; more than one-third of men and almost one-fifth of women reach orgasm in a homosexual encounter. Almost all men and women experience petting, some to orgasm. Coitus is the main adult outlet but half the total outlet of men as a whole does not come from marital coitus. Sexual contact with animals provides under 1% of total outlet, and our diagrams do not show it separately.

## Growth of experience

Kinsey's figures suggest more than three in four males have experienced at least four kinds of sexual activity by 25. By the same age fewer than one in five females have had an equal amount of experience. By the age of 50 less than half of all men and women have had any homosexual experience, and most women have had no sex dreams with orgasm.

## Male experience

The first of these graphs shows percentages of males who have experienced five kinds of sexual activity (with or without orgasm) at least once by given ages from under 10 to 50.

a Intercourse.
b Masturbation.
c Nocturnal sex dreams.
d Petting.
e Homosexuality.

## Female experience

The second graph shows percentages of females who have experienced five kinds of sexual activity (with or without orgasm) at least once by given ages, from 5 to 50.

1 Petting.
2 Intercourse.
3 Masturbation.
4 Nocturnal sex dreams.
5 Lesbianism (homosexuality).

# Average sexual experience

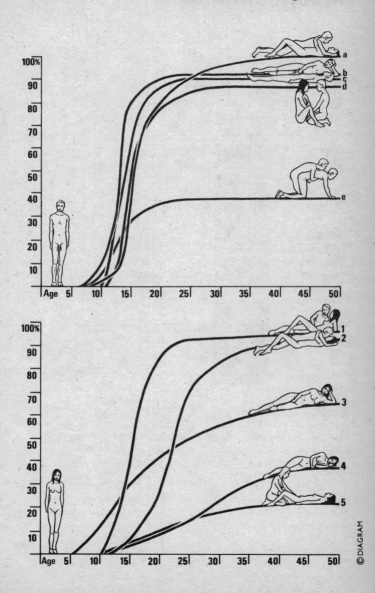

# Sexual outlets 2

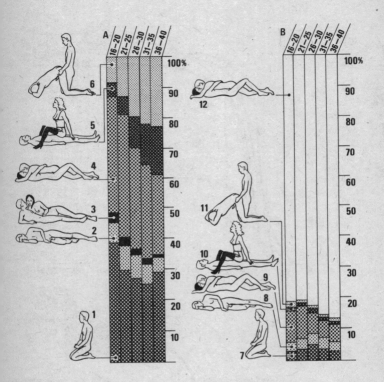

## A  Outlets of single men

Outlet ratios alter with age.
Masturbation declines as coital
outlet increases. The apparent
rise in homosexuality reflects
heterosexuals lost to marriage.
1  Masturbation.
2  Nocturnal sex dreams.
3  Petting to orgasm.
4  Nonmarital intercourse.
5  Intercourse with prostitutes.
6  Homosexuality.

## B  Outlets of married men

As a group, married men of all
ages get far more orgasms from
marital intercourse than all other
sources together. Other forms of
coitus rank next.
7  Masturbation.
8  Nocturnal sex dreams.
9  Nonmarital intercourse.
10  Intercourse with prostitutes.
11  Homosexuality.
12  Marital intercourse.

# Average sexual experience

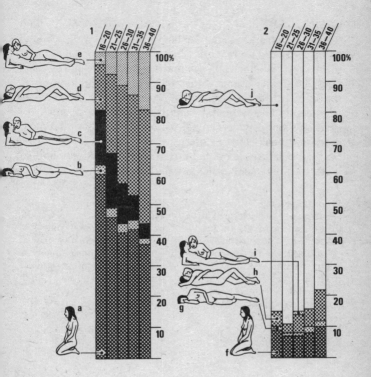

## 1 Outlets of single women

Masturbation and petting drop from first and second places to joint third and fourth place. Coitus and homosexuality rise to joint first and second place for the 36 to 40 age group.

**a** Masturbation.
**b** Nocturnal sex dreams.
**c** Petting to orgasm.
**d** Nonmarital intercourse.
**e** Homosexuality.

## 2 Outlets of married women

As with married men, marital outlet remains dominant at all ages. But other outlets increase from 15% to 22%. Research done since this Kinsey survey would rank extramarital sex higher.

**f** Masturbation.
**g** Nocturnal sex dreams.
**h** Extramarital sex.
**i** Homosexuality.
**j** Marital intercourse.

©DIAGRAM

217

# Sex and marriage 1

Marital intercourse accounts for 85% of married men's total sexual outlet, and sex in marriage is the only kind approved by all legal and moral codes. Yet 33-50% of marriages fail in some way. Satisfaction with marriage tends to fade as years pass. This can happen if the arrival of children loosens sexual bonds between parents. Also, differing sexual needs of husband and wife may lead to friction. For instance, a woman's sex drive is typically more varied than that of a man, and peaks later in life.

Many a marriage is helped if partners can talk over and so learn to satisfy each other's sexual needs.

### Precoital petting

This tends to be briefer inside than outside marriage, because marriage has fewer barriers to coitus itself. Highly educated people pet longer. Kinsey gives the following percentages for couples taking various times.

**a** Less than 3 minutes: 11%.
**b** 4-10 minutes: 33%.
**c** 11-20 minutes: 33%.
**d** Over 20 minutes: 22%.

### Frequency of coitus

This diagram indicates weekly frequency of marital coitus for four age groups, with a marked age-related decline. Based on a 1974 survey (Hunt), it shows more activity at all ages than did Kinsey's earlier surveys.

**A** 18-24 years: 3.25 times.
**B** 25-34 years: 2.55 times.
**C** 35-44 years: 2.00 times.
**D** 45 years and over: 1.00 time.

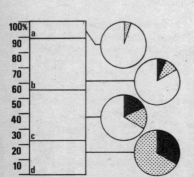

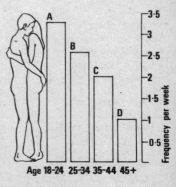

# Average sexual experience

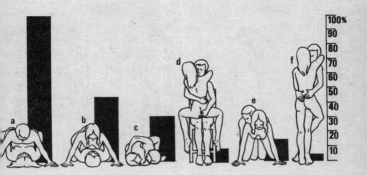

**Coital positions** (*above*)
Shown here are percentages of women who had tried six coital positions in marriage. Varying positions is now commoner than these Kinsey figures suggest.

**a** Male above 100%.
**b** Female above 45%.
**c** Side by side facing 31%.
**d** Sitting 9%.
**e** Rear entry 15%.
**f** Standing 4%.

**Marital coitus as an outlet** (*below*)
Here we see marital coitus as a percentage of total sexual outlet for married women (**A**) and men (**B**). This survey suggests a 5% and 17% decline respectively among men and women between 30 and 60. In men of high educational level the drop may be 23%, but among men of a low educational level marital coitus as a proportion of total outlet rises by 10%.

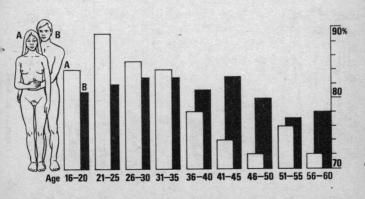

Age 16–20 21–25 26–30 31–35 36–40 41–45 46–50 51–55 56–60

©DIAGRAM

# Sex and marriage 2

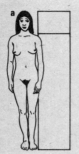
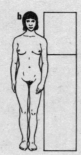

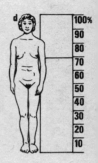

100%
90
80
70
60
50
40
30
20
10

**Decline in satisfaction** (*above*)
A 1975 survey (Levin & Levin) suggests women find marital sex less satisfying after the first few months, then reach a stable, if lower, level of satisfaction. After varying times, satisfaction was reported as follows.
**a** Less than 1 year: 82%.
**b** 1-4 years: 68%.
**c** 5-10 years: 67%.
**d** Over 10 years: 67%.

**Extramarital intercourse** (*below*)
This diagram shows incidence of extramarital intercourse among women (**A**) and men (**B**) in various age groups as listed by Kinsey. His surveys suggested that 26% of women and 50% of men were unfaithful at some time in their lives. Infidelity is now even commoner: some sexologists put infidelity for women at above 50%.

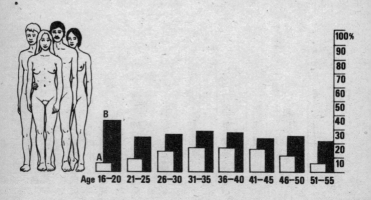

100%
90
80
70
60
50
40
30
20
10

Age 16-20  21-25  26-30  31-35  36-40  41-45  46-50  51-55

# Average sexual experience

**Unfaithful wives** (*above*)
Figures from a 1974 survey
(Redbook) show percentages of
married women, belonging to
different groups, who had had
extramarital sex.
a  Married under 1 year 12%.
b  Full-time housewives 27%.
c  Total unfaithful 30%.
d  Volunteer workers 32%.
e  Married over 10 years 38%.
f  Full-time wage earners 47%.

**Sex after marriage ends** (*below*)
More people than you might
think have sex after marriage ends.
The diagram shows percentages
among various age groups, based
on Kinsey's research. This also
found that 76%, 73% and 72% of
separated, divorced and
widowed women (respectively)
had sex at some time after their
marriage ended. More up-to-date
totals would possibly be over 90%.

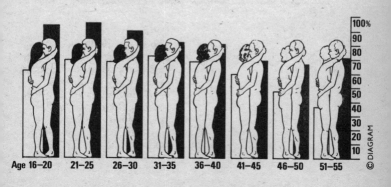

Age 16–20   21–25   26–30   31–35   36–40   41–45   46–50   51–55

© DIAGRAM

# Sexual capabilities 1

Sex drive and sexual abilities vary with age and between men and women (as well as with health in each person and among individuals of the same sex). Teenage boys have a strong sex drive, and some achieve eight orgasms a day. But teenage girls are less easily aroused. By their late 30s men want fewer orgasms than they did, but women tend to be quickly aroused and more likely than before to start intercourse. In both sexes the sexual drive grows less by old age. But 73% of men are still sexually potent at 70, and there is a psychological rather than physical reason why many others are not.

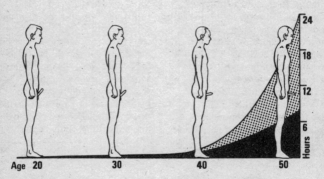

Age 20  30  40  50

Hours
24
18
12
6

**Refractory period**
The time elapsing after a man achieves one orgasm and before he can manage another is called the refractory period. In early teens this may last no more than seconds. Our diagram shows how the refractory period lengthens with age. By the late 30s it lasts half an hour. By the time a man is 50 his refractory period may last 8 to 24 hours.

# Average sexual experience

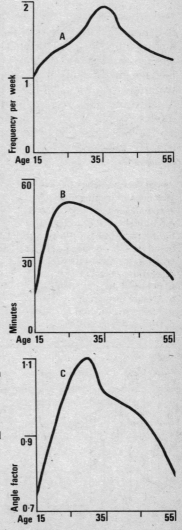

## A Morning erection
This graph shows how frequency of morning erection varies with age for males from 15 to 55. Recorded frequency rises from once weekly at 15 to twice that in the early 30s, then falls to below once weekly after 65. Despite this pattern, Kinsey estimated frequency to be highest of all in boys nearing or reaching adolescence.

## B Duration of erection
This graph shows how long males of different ages can keep up an erection if helped by some sort of erotic stimulus. In fact many teenagers can maintain an erection for hours with little physical stimulus; some even after several ejaculations. Few middle-aged men and no old ones can do this. Also, old men are slow to achieve an erection.

## C Angle of erection
The average angle (based on men of various ages) is just above the horizontal, but 45° or more in over one quarter of all men. In an individual male the angle tends to be highest in the early 20s and markedly lower after 50. Some old men claim to have experienced a drop from almost vertical in early manhood to below horizontal late in life.

# Sexual capabilities 2

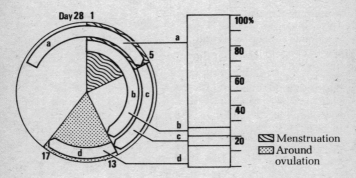

**Female sexual desire** (*above*)
Waxing and waning of female
sexual desire is related to the
monthly menstrual cycle. Our
figures (from *The Hite Report*) are
based on 436 women specifying
when in the month they felt an
increase in sexual desire.
**a** Before/at menstruation 74%.
**b** At/after menstruation 5%.
**c** After menstruation 7%.
**d** During ovulation 14%.

**Frequency of orgasm** (*below*)
This diagram (after Kinsey)
shows the median frequency of
orgasms per week for samples of
sexually active single men and
women of different ages. For
married people frequency was
greater — seven times greater for
married than unmarried women
of 16-20. In men frequency peaks
in the teens. In women it tends
to peak in the late 20s and 30s.

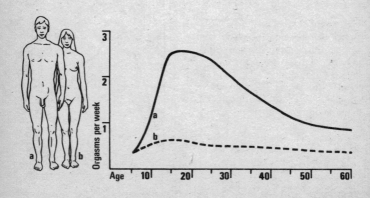

# Average sexual experience

 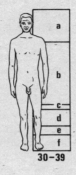  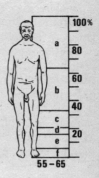

Age  18–29   30–39   40–54   55–65

**Male feelings about sex** (*above*)
A survey by Pietropinto asked over 4000 men how their feelings about sex had changed in the last five years. The diagram shows percentages who said they:
**a** felt the same about sex:
**b** enjoyed sex more than ever:
**c** found sex less enjoyable:
**d** varied sex practices more:
**e** found sex more routine:
**f** wanted more experiment.

**Multiple orgasm** (*below*)
This diagram, using research by Kinsey, shows percentages of sexually active females and males able to reach orgasm more than once in a session. About 14% of women achieve it, with little fall-off until their late 50s. In males it is achieved by over 50% of active preadolescents, but this figures falls rapidly and by age 25 is lower than for women.

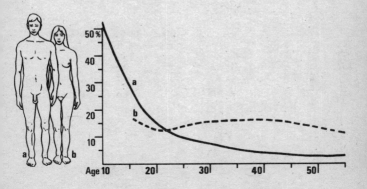

©DIAGRAM

225

# Sexual techniques 1

The items on these two pages give an idea of the enormous variety of sexual techniques and aids in use, besides the numerous possible intercourse positions (pp. 130-147). Most people achieve sexual release with help from a limited number of aids or techniques, and stick to these. Others experiment widely. A few individuals find arousal or reach orgasm in ways that the majority finds extraordinary. Those seeking new stimuli may be helped by commercially available devices like vibrators and pneumatic dolls, sex manuals, and pornographic magazines and movies.

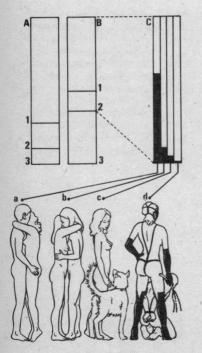

**Fantasy during masturbation**

Most individuals, but especially males, fantasize while masturbating. Heterosexuals have heterosexual fantasies, and so on for homosexuals, sado-masochists, and those with animal contacts. In the diagram *left*, bars **A** and **B** show the percentages of masturbating males and females who fantasize.

**A) Fantasies present (males)**
1 Almost always 72%.
2 Sometimes 17%.
3 Never 11%.

**B) Fantasies present (females)**
1 Almost always 50%.
2 Sometimes 14%.
3 Never 36%.

**C) Female fantasies**
Dark parts of narrow bars (**C**) show proportions of females who have various kinds of fantasy.
a Heterosexual 60%.
b Homosexual 10%.
c Animal 4%.
d Sadomasochistic 1%.

# Average sexual experience

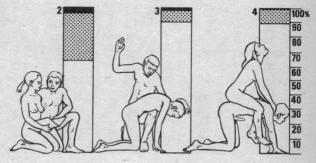

## Erotic aids (*above*)

Many items can trigger arousal. They include nude art, erotic stories, burlesque shows, erotic movies, dancing, and seeing or thinking about the opposite sex. Kinsey's surveys suggested: far more men than women respond to most items; equal arousal from reading literature; and a higher female than male response to being bitten in sex play. Figures here, from a late 1970s British survey, indicate percentages of women actively using various erotic aids.

**1** Clothing: 4% often; 20% sometimes; 76% never.
**2** Books/pictures: 4% often; 31% sometimes; 64% never.
**3** Spanking: 2% often; 8% sometimes; 90% never.
**4** Games: 1% often; 10% sometimes; 89% never.

■ Often
▨ Sometimes
□ Never

## Masturbation techniques (*below*)

Males mainly grip the penis and move the hand to and fro.
Women rub the clitoral area and use other techniques as follows.
**a** Fantasy alone 2%.
**b** Muscular tension 5%.
**c** Thigh pressure 10%.
**d** Breast stimulation 11%.
**e** Other methods 11%.
**f** Vaginal insertion 20%.
**g** Clitoral/labial massage 84%.

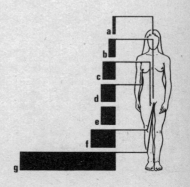

©DIAGRAM

# Sexual techniques 2

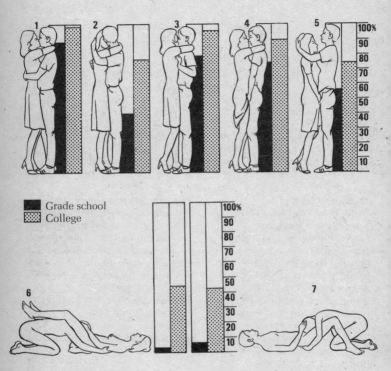

Grade school
College

## Petting techniques

Diagrams show percentages of men with grade school (0-8 years') and college (13+ years') education who had experienced various petting techniques (figures from Kinsey). Figures show those who were highly educated experimenting more in all items, but especially in items **6** and **7**. Items **1-5** occurred often and in marriage: **6** and **7** had simply occurred at some time.

**1** Lip kissing: 88% grade school, 98% college.
**2** Deep kissing: 40% grade school, 77% college.
**3** Hand on breast: 79% grade school, 96% college.
**4** Hand on her genitals: 75% grade school, 90% college.
**5** Hand on his genitals: 57% grade school, 90% college.
**6** Mouth to her genitals: 4% grade school, 45% college.
**7** Mouth to his genitals: 7% grade school, 43% college.

# Average sexual experience

## Sex in the dark

This diagram reveals lighting preferences during sex among males (1) and females (2).

**a** Much prefer light: 21% males, 8% females.

**b** Prefer some light: 19% males, 11% females.

**c** Prefer darkness: 35% males, 55% females.

**d** Do not have a preference: 25% males, 26% females.

## Sex nude

Attitudes to nudity in general vary greatly from culture to culture, and even between social classes in the same culture. Poorly educated people tend to think all nudity is obscene and most have intercourse clothed. No such inhibitions affect more highly educated people, who like nude intercourse for the tactile pleasure they get from close body-to-body contact.

Figures *below* show male and female preferences for nude sex related to educational levels. Since these Kinsey surveys more people have probably taken to having intercourse nude.

**1 Males preferring sex nude**

**a** Grade-school educated 43%.

**b** High-school educated 66%.

**c** College educated etc 89%.

**2 Females preferring sex nude**

**a** High-school educated 77%.

**b** College educated 89%.

**c** Postgraduates etc 90%.

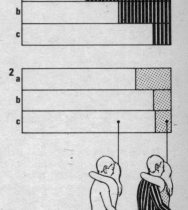

©DIAGRAM

229

# Attitudes to sex 1

Several surveys run in the 1970s tried to find out what men and women thought about sex in general and about special aspects of sex. These diagrams summarize findings published in *Beyond the Male Myth*, *The Hite Report*, and an article on married women by R.R. and P.L. Bell. Because male and female surveys were independent of each other they do not tally exactly. Then, too, totals mask age-based differences. For instance, twice as many men aged 18-29 wanted sex 3-7 times weekly as men aged 55-65. Moreover women showed a more sporadic desire for sex than their "desired frequency" figures suggest.

### A) Women's feelings about sex
Based on figures in *The Hite Report*, this first diagram shows how over 1600 American women replied when asked: do you like vaginal penetration/intercourse?
1 Yes 87%.
2 It's O.K. 2%.
3 Sometimes 4%.
4 Depends on partner 2%.
5 No 4%.

### B) Men's feelings about sex
Based on figures published in 1977 in *Beyond the Male Myth*, the next diagram shows how 4000 American men rated sex.
a Life's major pleasure 20%.
b Very important 61%.
c Important, showing love 11%.
d Just a physical pleasure 4%.
e Something you have to do 1%.
f Not very important to me 1%.
g Other things matter more 2%.

A

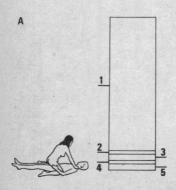

B

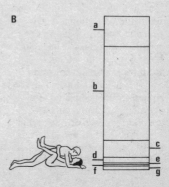

# Average sexual experience

## Desired frequency of coitus

This diagram shows how often men and women said they would ideally like to have sex when asked in two surveys late in the 1970s. Both surveys involved US citizens drawn from a range of age groups.

**1 Frequency desired by men**
**a** More than once a day 13%.
**b** 5-7 times a week 26%.
**c** 3-4 times a week 35%.
**d** 1-2 times a week 18%.
**e** 2-3 times a month 6%.
**f** Once a month or less 2%.

**2 Frequency desired by women**
**a** Once daily or more 30%.
**b** 3-5 times a week 16%.
**c** 2-3 times a week 16%.
**d** 1-2 times a week 15%.
**e** 3-4 times a month 1%.
**f** 1-2 times a month 3%.
**g** Often 7%.
**h** Varies 9%.
**i** Infrequently 2%.
**j** Never 1%.

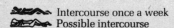
Intercourse once a week
Possible intercourse

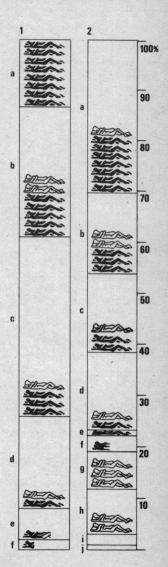

© DIAGRAM

231

# Attitudes to sex 2

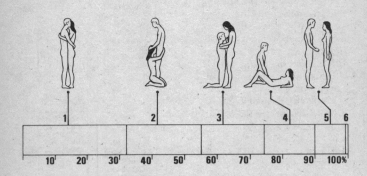

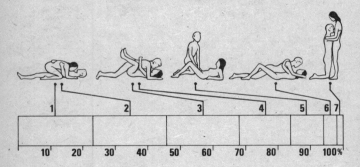

**What men like best** (*top*)
Our diagram reflects answers of
4752 American men asked what
foreplay they liked best. Most
enjoyed embrace without coitus
but few felt a real need for it.
1  Kissing and caressing 32%.
2  Oral sex 23%.
3  Touching her breasts 19%.
4  Touching her genitals 16%.
5  Seeing her nude body 9%.
6  Dislike foreplay 1%.

**What women like best** (*above*)
When 608 American women
were asked what they liked best
about sex they answered as
follows (some items are grouped).
1  Physical contacts 23%.
2  Reaching orgasm 23%.
3  Emotional intimacy 22%.
4  Sharing his pleasure 17%.
5  Pleasurable feelings 10%.
6  Intercourse 4%.
7  Foreplay 2%.

# Average sexual experience

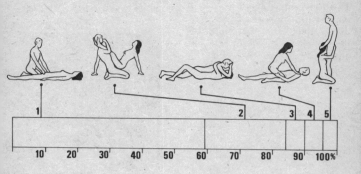

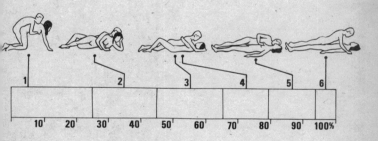

**What men like least** (*top*)
A survey of over 4000 American men asked what they found the most unpleasant aspect of sex. Given only the following five items to choose from, the men answered as follows.
1 Unresponsive woman 59%.
2 Odors and discharge 25%.
3 Feeling guilty 6%.
4 Demanding woman 6%.
5 Foreplay 4%.

**What women like least** (*above*)
More than 2400 women were asked which aspects of sex life they liked least. Nearly 2000 listed six main dislikes, given here in descending order.
1 Anal or oral sex 25%.
2 Messiness after sex 20%.
3 Lack of orgasm 20%.
4 Routine/ritual sex 14%.
5 Rough foreplay 14%.
6 Coitus 7%.

©DIAGRAM

233

# Chapter 10

This 19th century Flemish popular print uses a staircase to demonstrate stages in a couple's life, from birth to maturity and onward to old age.

TRAP DES OUDE

DEGRES DES AGES.

age de Maturite

age declinant

age de vieillesse

age caduc

age décrepitude

50 ans

60 ans

70 ans

80 ans

90 ans

age infantile

100 ans

JUGEMENT UNIVERSEL

# Sex in the later years 1

Although sexual topics are now much more openly discussed, the sexual needs and behavior of older people are often subject to considerable misunderstanding and even embarrassment. In society's eyes, and particularly among the young, it is still not considered "correct" for older people, who are probably parents and grandparents, to have the same sexual yearnings and desires as younger people. Such an attitude is ill-founded and grossly unfair and stems largely from society's current emphasis on youth and youthful attractiveness.

There is no doubt that the sex drive does decline with age. In men this decline starts in the twenties and then proceeds

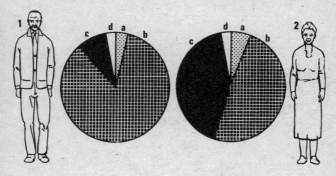

**Marital status and age**
Obviously a major factor in levels of sexual activity among older people is their marital status. This diagram, based on US Government statistics for 1975, shows the marital status of men and women in two older age groups. High percentages of women whose husbands have died reflect women's longer life expectancy and the fact that many marry older men.

gradually through life until about age sixty, when the rate of decline decreases. In women there is usually no appreciable decline at all until about age sixty, after which the rate of decline is very gradual. This picture is in no way consistent with the erroneous idea that old people should have no sex lives. People who enjoy sex earlier in life generally continue to do so as they get older, and although the aging process may make it necessary to adapt their lovemaking to some extent (see pages 244-245), most old people remain capable of intercourse for as long as their general health permits.

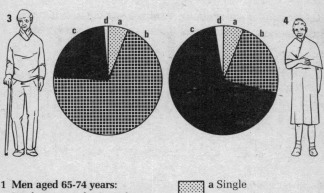

**1 Men aged 65-74 years:**
**a** Single 4%       **b** Married 84%
**c** Widowed 9%     **d** Divorced 3%
**2 Women aged 65-74 years:**
**a** Single 6%       **b** Married 49%
**c** Widowed 42%    **d** Divorced 3%
**3 Men aged 75 and over:**
**a** Single 6%       **b** Married 70%
**c** Widowed 23%    **d** Divorced 1%
**4 Women aged 75 and over:**
**a** Single 6%       **b** Married 23%
**c** Widowed 69%    **d** Divorced 2%

▨ **a** Single

▦ **b** Married

■ **c** Widowed

▢ **d** Divorced

©DIAGRAM

# Sex in the later years 2

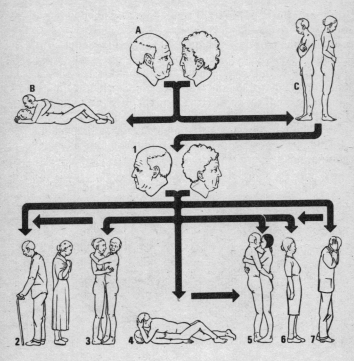

## Psychological problems

An older couple (**A**) with an enjoyable sex life (**B**) may find this threatened (**C**) by problems such as the following.

**1** Disharmony about nonsexual matters may disrupt the couple's physical relationship.

**2** An "old" attitude of mind may make the couple think they are too old for sex.

**3** The couple may still enjoy sex, but feel embarrassed about what others might think.

**4** Unimaginative lovemaking may lead to boredom with sex.

**5** Worry about declining sexual prowess may lead one partner to seek reassurance elsewhere, often with someone younger.

**6** Another response to fears of sexual decline is to reject sex completely.

**7** Worries about non-sexual matters — such as retirement or money — may interfere with sexual performance.

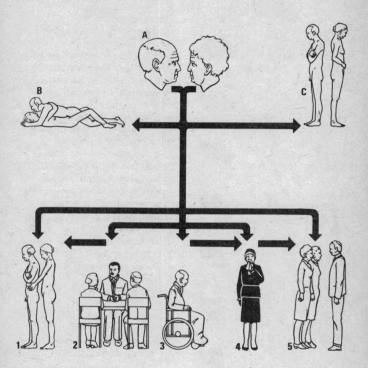

## Practical problems

Here we look at some of the practical problems that older people (**A**) may have to overcome if their enjoyment of sex (**B**) is not to come to an end (**C**).

**1** One partner may still be interested in sex but the other may not be.

**2** Physical problems associated with aging of the reproductive system (see pp. 240-243) may make intercourse uncomfortable unless they are treated.

**3** Ill health or infirmity may make intercourse difficult; trying special positions (see pp. 144-145, 147) may help.

**4** Death of one partner often ends the sex life of the other; many older people are not interested in finding a new mate.

**5** People who would like a new partner cannot always find one; women outnumber men in older age groups and some people are shy about meeting new people.

©DIAGRAM

# The aging process and sex 1

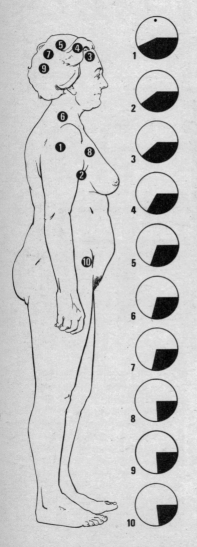

## The menopause

At the menopause, a woman's monthly menstrual cycle draws to a close: estrogen production by the ovaries is drastically reduced, eggs are no longer released for fertilization, and menstruation ceases. The first sign is usually irregularity of the periods. Many women also have various other symptoms and signs. Our diagram, based on Dutch and British surveys in the 1970s, shows percentages of women reporting some of the commonest menopausal (or climacteric) symptoms.

1 Fatigue 43%.
2 Night sweats 39%.
3 Headaches 38%.
4 Sleeplessness 32%.
5 Depression 30%.
6 Hot flashes (flushes) 29%.
7 Irritability 29%.
8 Palpitations 24%.
9 Dizziness 24%.
10 Formication — a sensation like ants on the skin 22%.

Here we describe some of the most important effects of the
aging process on the sex organs of women and men in
middle age and after. The physical changes described here
are all part of the natural aging process, and although there
may sometimes be problems to overcome there is generally
no need for them to bring sexual activity to an end.
For women, the most important developments at this time
are the hormonal and other changes related to the
menopause. The age of onset varies, but almost all women
have lost the capacity to bear children by age 55. For some
this is a traumatic and depressing experience, but for others

### Contraception

A woman of 50 plus is estimated
to be infertile 12 months after her
last period. To avoid any risk of
pregnancy, however, it is safer if
she continues using some type of
contraception for 2 years after her
last period. Women under 50
should certainly continue with
contraception for 2 years after
their periods stop.

### Postmenopausal changes

Reduced estrogen levels affect
the sex organs as follows. The
ovaries (**a**) and uterus (**b**) shrink.
Uterine muscle becomes fibrous
but is still probably contractile.
The vulva (**c**) atrophies. The
vaginal walls (**d**) get thinner. A
reduction in lubrication makes
the vagina liable to irritation, but
hormone creams counter this.

### Hormone replacement therapy

Severe menopausal symptoms
can be alleviated by means of
hormone replacement therapy
(HRT) but medical opinion on
the subject is deeply divided.
HRT generally consists of taking
pills to supplement the body's
natural supplies of estrogen,
sometimes in conjunction with
progesterone or androgen.

©DIAGRAM

# The aging process and sex 2

the menopause comes as a welcome relief. As a result of the menopause the sex organs do begin to show noticeable signs of aging, but most women should be able to remain as sexually active as they were before.

Few men experience a sudden loss of reproductive ability comparable with that in women, although the general aging process does bring noticeable changes to the sex organs. Sperm production also declines with age but there are cases of men in their nineties fathering children. Certainly impotence increases with age (see page 254), but very often the cause is psychological not physical.

**Physical changes in men**
Few men experience a sudden end to their reproductive potential comparable with that caused by the female menopause. For those who do, the causes are much more likely to be psychological than physical. By about age 60, however, the general aging process results in noticeable changes to the male sex organs.
**a** Hardening of blood vessels leading to erectile tissue in the penis makes it more difficult to obtain an erection.
**b** The scrotal tissue sags and wrinkles.
**c** The testes shrink and lose firmness, and their elevation on excitement is reduced.
**d** Thickening and degeneration of the seminiferous tubules inhibit production of sperm.
**e** The prostate gland often enlarges, and its contractions during orgasm become weaker.

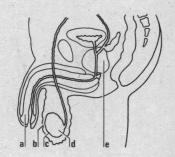

a  b  c  d      e

**Testosterone production**
In the typical male, production of the sex hormone testosterone peaks in early adulthood and then declines into old age. At around age 60, when the rate of decline slows down, the amount produced is similar to that of a 9 or 10 year old. Production usually remains sufficient for sexual activity to continue into extreme old age.

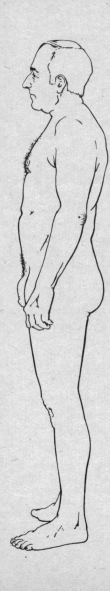

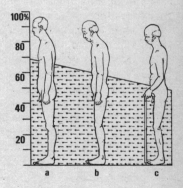

### Sperm in the ejaculate

Sperm production declines with age, but some very old men are known to have fathered children. Our diagram, based on research by V. Blum (1936), shows percentages of men in three older age groups who had sperm in their ejaculate.

**a** 60-70 years: 68.5%.
**b** 70-80 years: 59.5%.
**c** 80-90 years: 48%.

©DIAGRAM

243

# Continuing sexual activity 1

The ability to enjoy lovemaking can continue well into old age, particularly if a couple makes the effort to understand and respond to the various changes that age brings to the natural pattern of sexual response. All too often, older couples give up intercourse because they mistakenly interpret these changes as signs of forthcoming impotence. Lovemaking may have to become a more leisurely affair as a couple gets older, but the benefits of maintaining the physical side of a relationship into old age can be great.

**Older women** will probably find that their cycle of sexual response is much less affected by age than is that of their partner, although in women, too, sexual arousal does tend to take rather longer as they get older, and orgasm is typically more rapidly completed. The menopause does not usually reduce a woman's sex drive and even if it does, this effect is usually only temporary. Intercourse may, however, be made painful by vaginal dryness, thinning vaginal walls, and strong uterine contractions during orgasm — all these problems are directly caused by estrogen deficiency and can be alleviated with hormone pills or by using local applications (pessaries or creams).

**Older men** generally need a longer period of sexual excitement before an erection occurs. One survey found that men aged 48 to 65 took on average five times as long to achieve an erection as men aged 19 to 30. A man who could attain an erection in only a few seconds when he was young may find that he requires several minutes when he is older. Once an erection is achieved, however, an older man has the advantage of being able to maintain it for much longer. Feelings of ejaculatory inevitability tend to disappear with age, giving greater ejaculatory control and allowing the older man to prolong intercourse almost indefinitely if he adopts the technique of withdrawing temporarily whenever orgasm is imminent.

Although orgasm is reached more slowly by older men, orgasm itself is completed more quickly. Orgasmic contractions are no longer as strong, the force of ejaculation is reduced, and the seminal fluid is thinner and reduced in quantity. Even so, orgasm remains a pleasurable experience. After ejaculation the older man tends to lose his erection very quickly and it may be some time — hours or even days — before he is capable of another (see page 222). If a couple wants intercourse more often than the man's capacity for erection allows, he can use his greater ejaculatory control to avoid orgasm — further erections will then be no problem.

# Continuing sexual activity 2

**Age 60–64**   **65–69**   **70–74**   **75+**

**Comparisons of sexual activity**
These diagrams are based on a Duke University study of older people living in and around Durham, North Carolina. People taking part were volunteers and none was institutionalized. All with any degree of regularity or periodicity of intercourse were classed as "sexually active."

**1 Sexual activity by age**
The study showed comparatively little variation in percentages who were sexually active in the first three age groups (59%, 64%, 58%). But over 75 there was a big drop — usually attributed to illness — to only 26%.

**2 Men compared with women**
The level of sexual activity was higher among men (61%) than women (44%), but more women were widowed or had sick partners.

**3 By socio-economic status**
Those of low status had a higher level of sexual activity (66%) than those of high status (42%).

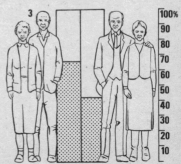

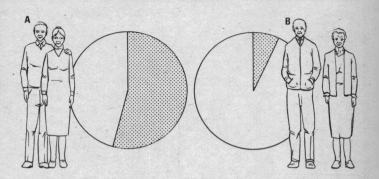

**Sex and marital status** (*above*)
Of persons taking part in the
North Carolina survey, sexual
activity was reported by 54% of
those who were married (**A**) and
by 7% of those who were single,
divorced or widowed (**B**).
Although the sex drive often
remains strong enough for sex to
continue within marriage, it is
not often strong enough to lead
to extramarital sex.

**Masturbation** (*below*)
These diagrams, using research
by Kinsey, show the importance
of masturbation as a sexual outlet
among older people.
**1** Among men over 60 years old,
25% masturbate regularly.
**2** Among unmarried women
aged 50-70, about 59% in the
Kinsey survey admitted to
masturbating.
**3** About 30% of older women
masturbate to supplement coitus.

# Chapter 11

A contemporary comment on the problems of interpersonal relations, by the cartoonist Bretécher.

# Sexual problems

# Mutual problems 1

Sexual problems of some kind affect most couples at one time or another. At least half of all US marriages reportedly suffer, and sexual difficulties affect at least three-quarters of all psychiatric patients.

Often one partner cannot or will not have sex in a way that the other enjoys. Perhaps the man cannot achieve or maintain an erection. Or he may reach orgasm too soon for the woman. Some women complain that they never reach orgasm. Others find intercourse distasteful or boring. Occasionally a man or woman suffers pain during intercourse: a local infection may be to blame. Physical causes also underlie some other sexual problems. But most have psychological roots, often traceable to unhealthy attitudes to sex instilled in childhood.

Where sex occurs casually, sexual failure may not lastingly damage the couple involved. But if both share an enduring commitment, the harm may strike deeply. An individual's own failure may injure self-esteem badly enough to sour that person's outlook on life, blighting even non-sexual relationships. Then, too, one partner may blame the other. The resulting discord accounts for many divorces.

Most sex therapists insist that in every committed relationship any sexual problem and its solution must involve both partners. Thus the influential sex therapy of Masters and Johnson hinges on both troubled partners cooperating to cure what may appear to be sexual inadequacy in only one of the pair. The therapist or therapists (often a male and a female specialist who work as a team) encourage the couple to hold so-called sensate-focus therapy sessions: the sexually inadequate person learns to enjoy touching the partner, until sexual hang-ups give way to a healthy attitude to sexual intercourse as something both can share and enjoy.

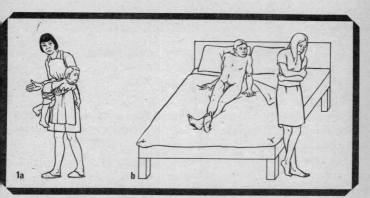

## Two causes of inadequacy

**1a** Discouraging a young child's healthy interest in sex can create mental blocks causing sexual inadequacy later in life.

**b** Even the sexually successful performer may fail if he or she becomes over self-conscious, and fearful of failure. Fear upsets the body's rhythm so that real failure may follow, perhaps time after time.

## Treating inadequacy

**2a** The inadequate person learns to feel and caress all of the partner's body while both lie unclothed on a bed or couch.

**b** A special lotion softens the hands, making their touch both smoother and more sensitive. The lotion also helps to rid the user of inhibitions about the similarly textured sexual fluids: vaginal secretions and semen.

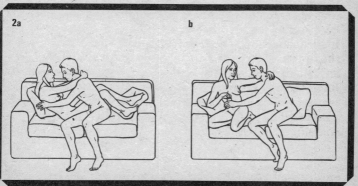

© DIAGRAM

# Mutual problems 2

## Sex and family life

**A** Good sexual relations between husband and wife help to promote good general relationships between each other and between them and their children.

**B** Poor sexual relations between husband and wife spill over into daily life to produce poor everyday relationships between them and between them and their children. The cause of the trouble may be physical but most sexual difficulties are psychological in origin. In time one frustrated partner may reject sex entirely, or one or both may seek satisfaction outside marriage. So if the partners fail to grasp its importance, what had seemed to be a problem affecting just a brief part of family life can threaten its very foundations.

Sex therapy helps couples to understand and tackle many sexual problems. In most cases success rates are high.

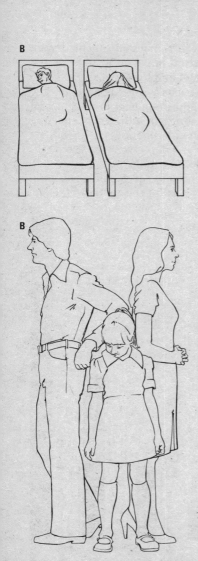

# Impotence 1

Impotence is failure to achieve or maintain an erection for intercourse. Almost all men are impotent at some time. About 10 per cent are impotent for physical reasons. These include genital or central nervous system defects present from birth. Physical causes appearing later in life include: certain diseases, hormonal disorders and surgery affecting the genital organs; any major chronic illness; overdependence on alcohol, antidepressants and some other drugs; fatigue; and poor nutrition.

About 90 per cent of impotence has a psychological cause, ranging from conscious fear of failure or dislike of the

**Incidence of impotence**
This diagram shows that the incidence of impotence increases with age. Up to middle age fewer than 10 per cent of men are affected, compared with almost all 90-year-olds. This picture can be misleading, for many old men enjoy sex occasionally. (A man is held to be impotent if one in four sexual attempts fails to produce an erection.)

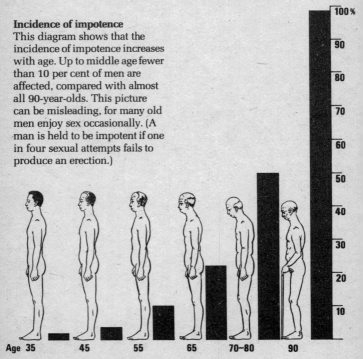

Age 35    45    55    65    70–80    90

partner to a dislike of sex or resentment of women deeply rooted in some childhood maladjustment. Men with this last type of problem may never have had an orgasm. But some men impotent with their wives can masturbate or have sexual intercourse with a mistress.

Therapy can show a man how to enjoy body contact with his partner without feeling he must achieve an erection to order. In due course he probably will. (Masters and Johnson reported success with more than 7 in 10 of temporarily impotent men, and with about 6 in 10 of men who had always been impotent.)

### Primary impotence

This term covers men who have never achieved or sustained an erection. Common causes are:

**A** a homosexual liaison of a year or more;

**B** undue maternal influence with strong sexual overtones;

**C** a traumatic first sexual experience, often a seamy, dehumanizing encounter with a prostitute.

A

B

C

# Impotence 2

**Secondary impotence**
Previously potent men become impotent for many reasons.

**1** The commonest cause is consistently reaching orgasm too soon for the woman. In time her complaints make the man avoid sex altogether. When he finally tries again he cannot produce an erection. This failure fuels self-fulfilling fears of more failures to follow.

**2** A lifestyle that features a large intake of alcohol is the second commonest cause of secondary impotence. Typically, a husband fails to produce an erection while trying to make love to a wife antagonized by his recent drunken behavior. Later attempts also fail through fear and anxiety and the effects on his body of too many drinks, taken to help him relax.

**3** A domineering mother or father is the third commonest cause of secondary impotence. A man who had been unhealthily close to his mother may reject sex because subconsciously he sees his wife as his mother. Secondary impotence also often stems from repressive religious teaching, an inner clash between heterosexual and homosexual impulses, or poor sex education.

### Impotence therapy

Impotence therapy is aimed at
removing both partners' fear of
the man's failure by involving
him in pleasurable sensations of
tactile give and take, as the
woman reassures and physically
stimulates him.

**A** Each partner fondles the
other's breasts and genitals. Each
time an erection occurs the man
lets it subside.

**B** Only after 10 days or so of
foreplay of the kind described
should the couple try sexual
intercourse. The wife kneels over
the man and steers his penis into
her vagina, moving her hips. If
the penis grows limp they start
again. Once the penis can stay
erect inside the vagina, the man
does all the thrusting. If the
couple are truly relaxed orgasm
will follow.

### Artificial penis (C)

Therapy is useless for men who
are physically incapable of an
erection. Now, however, even
these may be helped. Treatment
consists of an operation in which
a surgeon implants a silicone rod
in the penis. The rod keeps the
penis stiff during intercourse,
and the body does not reject the
silicone as it might a biological
transplant.

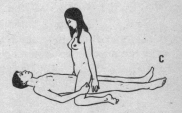

©DIAGRAM

# Ejaculatory problems 1

According to one British study, the commonest obstacle to sexual enjoyment is a woman's frustration caused by a man who ejaculates before she is sexually satisfied. Early ejaculation is common with men new to sexual intercourse. But an American survey suggests that three-quarters of all men ejaculate less than two minutes after inserting the penis in the vagina. The problem of so-called premature ejaculation arises only when ejaculation is so frequently too soon for the woman that the emotional quality of the sexual union suffers, and she may seek medical help or new sexual outlets.

Fortunately, premature ejaculation is usually easy to treat. Help with an abnormally sensitive penis or some other physical problem assists a few men. Others may find that intercourse soon after orgasm delays ejaculation. Because ejaculation is controlled by the brain and spinal cord, men may also fend it off with unsexy thoughts of, say, mortgage repayments. But since persistent premature ejaculation has an emotional or psychological basis it is often best dealt with by therapy that removes the fear and anxiety built up by past failures. Masters and Johnson have claimed a success rate of almost 98% for their own methods, outlined on page 259.

While many men ejaculate too soon, a far smaller number fail to ejaculate at all during intercourse. Some of these succeed by masturbating, or with a homosexual partner or a woman other than their wife. Ejaculatory incompetence stems from conscious or unconscious fears perhaps derived from some forgotten emotional trauma.

As in premature ejaculation, treatment depends on both partners' willing cooperation to overcome one partner's sexual inadequacy. Masters and Johnson's therapy, outlined on pages 260-261, is likely to succeed with at least four out of five couples who try it.

### Early ejaculation: causes

Backseat or sofa teenage sexual encounters, hurried by fear of discovery, can set a pattern of premature ejaculation that persists into adulthood. Other causes include hurrying by a prostitute; the birth-control method of withdrawal, or coitus interruptus; and selfishness by men intent only on sexually gratifying themselves.

### Reducing tension

Muscular tension is one cause of premature ejaculation, especially when intercourse happens in cramped conditions, such as on a small sofa or on the backseat of an automobile. But if the man lies beneath the woman, playing a fairly inactive role, he suffers less from muscular tension and is therefore less liable to ejaculate prematurely.

### Therapy

She masturbates him until just before he feels ejaculation is inevitable. Then she squeezes the head of the penis rather hard for 3-4 seconds, and his urge to ejaculate goes. The stimulation and squeezing go on for 15-20 minutes. Later she kneels over him for intercourse and he withdraws for squeezing until this becomes unnecessary.

© DIAGRAM

# Ejaculatory problems 2

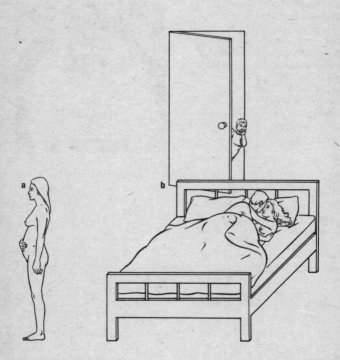

**Incompetence: causes**
Fear of making the woman
pregnant (**a**), and fear that the
children will walk in during
intercourse (**b**) are conscious
fears that can stop ejaculation.
Other possible factors include
dislike of the woman or knowing
that she has been unfaithful. Her
willingness to help him solve his
problem can help to repair a
damaged relationship.

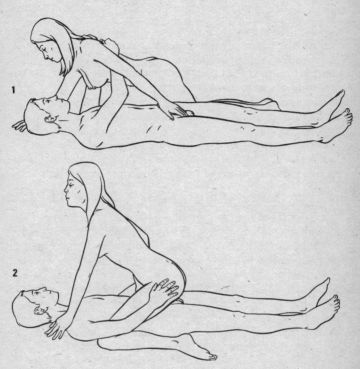

### Incompetence therapy

**1** The woman masturbates the man or otherwise makes him ejaculate outside her vagina. It may help if she uses a lotion similar to vaginal secretions. By giving him pleasure and showing she wants to do so she improves the couple's damaged relationship and paves the way for the next stage in overcoming his ejaculatory incompetence.

**2** The second stage is for the woman to kneel over her partner and again bring him to orgasm outside her vagina. Once he feels orgasm is inevitable she quickly inserts his penis in her vagina so that he ejaculates at least some of his semen inside her. After they have repeated this process several times the couple can achieve ejaculation entirely inside her vagina.

© DIAGRAM

# Non-orgasmic women 1

Sexual inadequacy among women chiefly takes the form of failure to reach orgasm. Some societies do not recognize that women need this sexual climax. But repeated congestion of genital organs without relief via orgasm brings discomfort, frustration and psychological damage.

Sometimes the cause is the man's impotence or ineptitude. If the trouble lies in the woman it may be organic: perhaps inborn defects of the sexual system; imbalance of hormones; or injury or inflammation affecting the genitals. She may suffer the effects of nervous disorders; overindulgence in drink or drugs; or loss of sexual drive through stress or aging.

Psychological causes are by far the commonest. The woman may resent the man as sexually unattractive, selfish or stupid; for his low income; or as a poor substitute for a man she prefers. Mentally, then, she rejects him as a sexual mate and makes this evident by her dismaying lack of sexual response.

Some "frigid" women were taught as children that — as one writer puts it — "sex is bad, wrong and dirty." Such notions warp these women's attitude to sex so that they view with guilt, fear and shame their own sexual feelings and try to suppress them, remaining sexually unresponsive if they marry. Other (often related) psychological blocks are emotional ties with the father; subconscious hatred of men; fear of pregnancy; and fear of pain on intercourse.

But some women fail because they are actually overeager to succeed, and so too tense to reach orgasm.

Treating the non-orgasmic woman involves considerate, stimulating sex play when she is relaxed and both partners are in harmony. The Masters and Johnson method has brought orgasm in 83% of women who had never had it and 77% of those who had lost orgasmic ability.

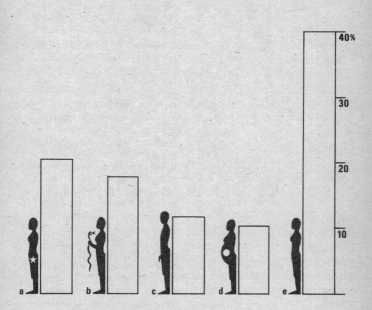

**Unconsummated marriage**
A survey of 1000 women with unconsummated marriages revealed the following reasons:
**a** sex too painful (20.3%);
**b** sex nasty (17.8%);
**c** husband impotent (11.7%);
**d** fear of pregnancy or childbirth (10.2%);

**e** other things, eg vagina too small, ignorance, lesbianism, penis phobia (40%).
Early sex education would have stopped most problems arising.

©DIAGRAM

# Non-orgasmic women 2

**1 Stimulation techniques**

**a** Considerate caressing by the man when the woman is feeling relaxed may help to arouse her. He should find which areas she most likes to have stroked. Periods of rest should punctuate attempts at arousal. Tenderly telling the woman he loves her will usually make her far more responsive than roughly seizing and manipulating her.

**b** A non-orgasmic woman seeking arousal sometimes finds it helpful to concentrate her mind upon some sexual fantasy. Reading erotic books and looking at erotic magazines may assist her. Meanwhile the man can encourage her with words of endearment to show that she gives him pleasure. Talking about sexually stimulating topics works with some women.

**c** Masturbation by vibrator or by hand may help to stimulate some women who can be aroused yet are sexually less sensitive than most. Other physical aids include deep penetration by the penis, and oral-genital contact. The man can reinforce physical efforts with encouraging words. Any method that brings orgasm once makes it easier for a woman to reach more orgasms later.

## 2 Sensate-focus therapy

**a** The couple sit nude on their bed: the man, legs apart, propped up by the headboard; the woman seated with her back to his chest and her legs on his. She guides his hands briefly over her inner thighs, vaginal lips and clitoral region. In this way she can control her sexual sensations and stop them becoming too intense for her.

**b** In subsequent sessions the couple eventually work up to the point where the woman kneels astride the man and finds pleasure in keeping still with his penis inside her vagina. She can then try slowly moving her hips to and fro, thrusting faster and harder when she finds that she wants to. Next she has him join in with his own thrusting hip movements.

**c** The last part of this Masters and Johnson therapy is shifting from the woman-on-top position to both partners lying sideways, so she rests largely on her chest, stomach, one leg, and the knee of the other leg. This position makes uncontrolled hip movements easier and orgasm likelier for women than positions where they can consciously control the movements made by their bodies.

# Painful intercourse 1

Men or women may suffer pain on intercourse. Different
sorts of pain come from trouble in different sites.
In men, sharp stabbing pain from the penis tip may mean
trouble there or in the prostate gland. A widespread pelvic
ache derived from the prostate gland, and aching testes are
other features. A burning feeling may come from the
bladder, prostate, or seminal vesicles.
Women may suffer superficial irritation or pain from the
clitoris. Aching, burning or itching may affect the vagina.
Severe "deep" pain affecting other internal organs includes
a sickening sensation involving damage to uterus or ovaries.

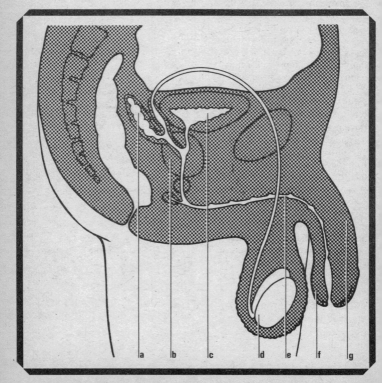

A common cause of pain on intercourse is infection. Vaginal douches indirectly help germs invade the vagina. Men who do not wash beneath the foreskin can get infections of the penile glans. Venereal disease may lead to inflammation. Sensitivity of the penis, clitoris or vagina to certain substances can set up irritation. Tissue injury produced by operation, rape or accident can be another cause of pain on intercourse.

Depending on the cause of the trouble, antibiotics, hormone drugs, washing, irritant avoidance, or surgery will usually solve the problem.

### Pain in men on intercourse

Male sites of pain and reasons for it include the following.

**a** Seminal vesicles: infection.

**b** Prostate: inflammation caused by infection; overenlargement; cancer; or — in old men — spasmodic contractions just before orgasm.

**c** Bladder: infection.

**d** Testes: unrelieved congestion caused by prolonged erection without ejaculation.

**e** Urethra: adhesions caused by gonorrhea in the urethra.

**f** Glans penis: pain due to a build-up of smegma and germs; adhesion of glans to a too-tight foreskin; inflamed urethra or prostate; or contact with germs, acid or contraceptive cream in the vagina.

**g** Shaft of penis: on erection is painfully bowed up and bent sideways (Peyronie's disease); on erection is painfully bowed down (chordee); pain due to badly performed circumcision.

©DIAGRAM

# Painful intercourse 2

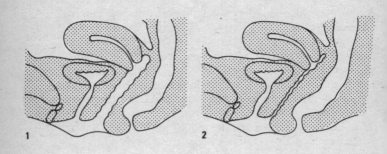

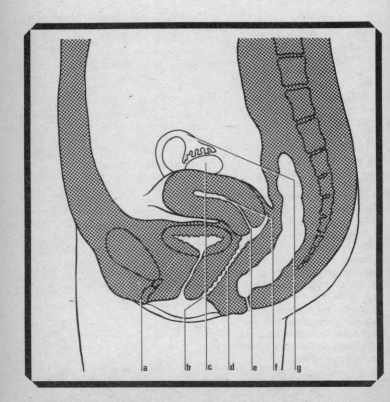

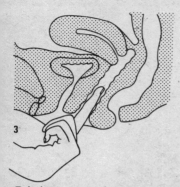

**3**

## Pain in women on intercourse

Female sites and conditions include the following.

**a** Clitoris: pain due to smegma, infection, or injury as when a man directly rubs the clitoris.

**b** Vaginal outlet: scars or tears linked with first intercourse, IUD strings, rape, abortion or childbirth; atrophy due to aging.

**c** Ovaries: inflammation, displacement, or cysts.

**d** Vagina: lack of lubrication due to lack of involvement in sex or lack of estrogen; infection due to a lowering of vaginal acidity caused by for example douches allowing invasion of germs via fingers, penis etc; sensitivity to rubber devices.

**e** Cervix inflamed by infection or "spilt" bits of womb lining causing fibrous growths in the genital system (endometriosis).

**f** Uterus: inflammation (as **e**), displacement, or torn ligaments.

**g** Fallopian tubes: as **e**.

## Vaginismus

**1** The muscles surrounding the vagina are usually relaxed enough at intercourse to let a penis enter the vagina.

**2** In some women muscular spasm contracts the muscles so that the vagina and its opening are narrowed. Called vaginismus, this condition makes intercourse difficult. If the contraction is very strong and lasts for hours attempts at intercourse produce excruciating pain in the woman and the penis is quite shut out. Vaginismus often happens in a woman frustrated by an impotent husband's failed attempts at intercourse. Fear, guilt, or expectation of pain — linked with a physical problem, past rape or a lesbian tendency — can also cause vaginismus. The ill-educated poor are least affected.

**3** Sex therapists often advise stretching the vaginal muscles by inserting progressively larger dilators into the vagina over three to five days, and, once the largest fits, keeping it in overnight. (Some women use their fingers for dilation.) Failure of physical methods may mean a need for psychotherapy. Almost all patients profit from some kind of treatment.

©DIAGRAM

# Chapter 12

1 *Mors Syphilitica*, part of an etching by the Belgian artist Félicien Rops (1833-1898).
2 A recruit for the brothel is greeted by the disease-ridden madam — from William Hogarth's *A Harlot's Progress*, 1732 (British Museum).

# Incidence and prevention 1

These infectious diseases are spread mainly by sexual contact, for their germs thrive in the moist, warm linings of genitals, rectum or mouth. Many produce only local irritation. A few can kill if untreated.

There are five notifiable types of venereal disease (VD), so-called for Venus, Roman goddess of love. Syphilis and gonorrhea have a rising worldwide incidence. Chancroid, lymphogranuloma venereum and granuloma inguinale are tropical and less widespread than they were.

Other sexual infections include nonspecific urethritis, trichomoniasis, genital candidosis, genital herpes, genital warts and molluscum contagiosum. Most show signs of

**Prevalence in the USA**
Compared here is the relative prevalence of 13 sexually transmitted diseases among persons visiting US venereal clinics in the late 1970s. Figures show the number of women (w) and men (m) diagnosed as suffering from each of these diseases for every 100 clinic visits by persons of each sex. The USA has one of the highest levels of sexual disease. In 1977 gonorrhea was nearly five times commoner than chicken pox, the second commonest notifiable disease. Gonorrhea cases far exceeded the official 1 million. Over half a million Americans may have syphilis and 5 million may suffer genital herpes.

**a** Gonorrhea 15.0 (w), 24.0 (m).
**b** Nonspecific genital infections 11.3 (w), 24.8 (m).
**c** Trichomoniases 10.4 (w).
**d** Candidoses 6.1 (w).
**e** Molluscum contagiosum 3.4 (w), 1.0 (m).
**f** Genital warts 3.0 (w), 4.3 (m).
**g** Genital herpes 1.5 (w), 3.4 (m).
**h** Syphilis 1.4 (w), 1.7 (m).
**i** Scabies 0.4 (w), 1.3 (m).
**j** Crab lice 1.6 (w), 2.9 (m).
**k** Chancroid 0.1 (w), 0.1 (m).
**l** Lymphogranuloma venereum 0.0 (w), < 0.1 (m).
**m** Granuloma inguinale 0.0 (w), 0.0 (m).

increase. Also several "non-sexual" diseases — a few
possibly serious — have proved mainly sexual in origin.
More men than women catch venereal diseases. These are
especially found among male homosexuals and prostitutes.
But the promiscuous young of either sex and of any social
class, religion or race are highly at risk.
Modern medicine can cure most sexual diseases. Yet some
are commoner than ever. Reasons include increased
promiscuity; declining use of condoms; more travel by
young unattached people; and new disease strains that
resist treatment or produce symptomless carriers.

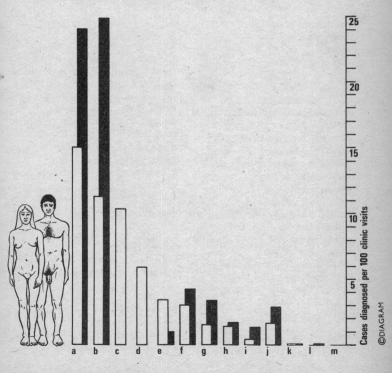

Cases diagnosed per 100 clinic visits

©DIAGRAM

# Incidence and prevention 2

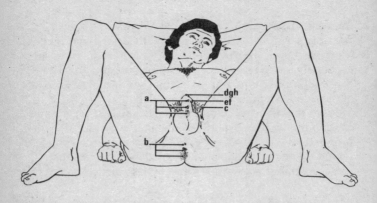

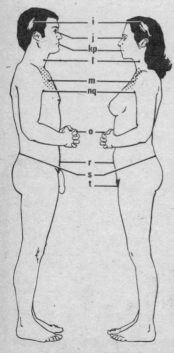

**Signs and symptoms**

These diagrams indicate signs and symptoms of some sexually spread diseases in men and women. Other conditions may produce similar effects. If in doubt always seek treatment.

**Genital area signs and symptoms:**

**a** A sore, ulcer or rash on the penis, vagina or vulval lips.

**b** A sore, ulcer or rash on or near the anus.

**c** Swollen glands in the groin.

**d** A burning sensation or pain on urination.

**e** An itchy or sore vagina or an itchy penis tip.

**f** Pain on intercourse.

**g** Unusual discharge from the penis or vagina.

**h** A frequent urge to urinate.

**Signs and symptoms elsewhere:**

**i** Patchy hair loss.

**j** Eye infection.

**k** A sore, ulcer or rash in the mouth or on the lips.

**l** A sore throat after fellatio.

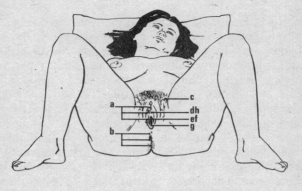

**m** Body rash.

**n** Sores in soft skin folds.

**o** A rash, sore or ulcer on finger or hand.

**Related conditions** from internal spread of disease include:

**p** Nausea.

**q** Low-grade fever.

**r** Abdominal pain.

**s** Low backache.

**t** Excessive, painful periods.

## Treating infection

**1** If you suspect you have a sexually transmitted disease have a confidential medical examination as soon as possible.

**2** If infected, warn your sex partner(s) to seek medical aid.

**3** Avoid sexual contact.

**4** Follow treatment prescribed.

**5** When cured have repeat tests to make sure.

**6** Avoid reinfection.

## Preventing infection

The following all reduce risk of infection. (Vaccines may also be available some day.)

**1** Wash genitals daily.

**2** Change underwear daily. Avoid underwear made of nylon.

**3** Avoid contact with chemicals that irritate the genitals.

**4** Wipe the bottom from front to back (especially women).

**5** Keep sexual contact to one partner free from infection.

**6** If changing partners leave 6 weeks between to give any major infection time to show up.

**7** Look for discharge or sores on a new partner's genitals.

**8** Use a condom at intercourse. Contraceptive creams, foams etc also help block infection.

**9** Wash genitals before and after intercourse.

**10** Urinate after intercourse.

©DIAGRAM

# Syphilis 1

Syphilis is the gravest and most feared venereal disease.
First symptoms are slight and may pass unnoticed. But
untreated syphilis may irreversibly damage vital organs,
causing blindness, insanity, paralysis and death.
In most countries syphilis is usually spread by penis or
vagina, less often by tongue, (cut) finger, mouth or rectum.
But endemic syphilis — found in Arabia and parts of Africa
— may be transmitted by cups or spoons.
Untreated syphilis passes through four stages which may
span altogether more than 30 years. The first, second and
fourth (late) stage show active signs of disease (for details
see captions and diagrams). The third — latent — stage lacks

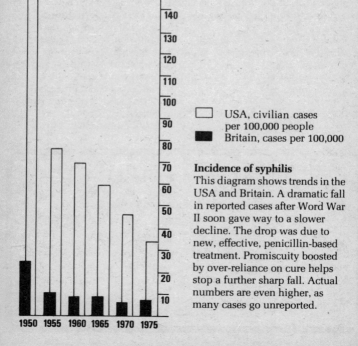

☐ USA, civilian cases
per 100,000 people
■ Britain, cases per 100,000

**Incidence of syphilis**
This diagram shows trends in the
USA and Britain. A dramatic fall
in reported cases after Word War
II soon gave way to a slower
decline. The drop was due to
new, effective, penicillin-based
treatment. Promiscuity boosted
by over-reliance on cure helps
stop a further sharp fall. Actual
numbers are even higher, as
many cases go unreported.

symptoms, and victims may then seem healthy. The latent stage starts six months to two years after infection and lasts up to 30 years.

This disease is easily treated if diagnosed before irreversible damage occurs. Even when no germs can be seen, the body's response to their presence betrays them, though not all tests are infallible; some may produce positive results from other diseases or vaccination. Treatment is by the injection of penicillin or another antibiotic, followed by medical checks. Luckily syphilis does not seem to be gaining immunity to penicillin.

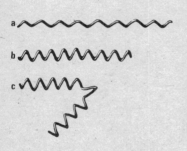

### The syphilis bacterium

*Treponema pallidum* is an unusual spiral-shaped bacterium that was discovered in 1905. It stretches (**a**) and contracts (**b**) like a spring; bends at more than a right angle (**c**); and corkscrews forward or backward. It can divide once every 30 hours. Similar spirochetes (spiral bacteria) cause the tropical diseases bejel, pinta and yaws.

### The primary sore

This most often occurs on a man's glans penis or foreskin or on a woman's vulval lips or clitoris. It starts as a small red spot that grows moist and eroded, with a hard base that feels like a button. It may be almost too small to see or the size of a fingernail. Treating with ointment is useless for germs have invaded the body.

# Syphilis 2

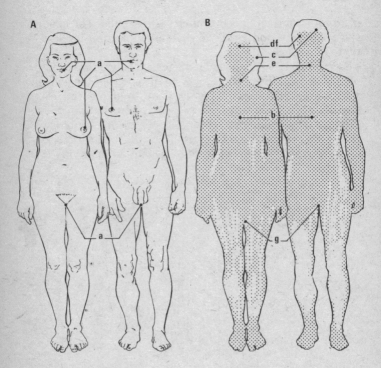

## A) First stage syphilis

Usually 10 to 40 days after infection a painless sore (**a**) appears on the area that had been directly infected. Besides the genital area this can be at the anus, on the lips or on a nipple. Nearby glands may be swollen. The chancre (sore) clears up on its own within 4 to 10 weeks. At the first stage a complete cure is easily made.

## B) Second stage syphilis

From 6 weeks to 3 months after infection a skin rash (**b**) appears, and patches of hair (**c**) drop out. There may be headache (**d**), sore throat (**e**), a slight fever (**f**) and swollen glands (**g**). Sufferers are very infectious and can transmit the disease by kissing if the skin of the mouth is broken. All signs of disease vanish within a year at most.

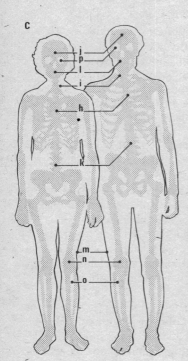

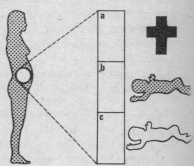

## C) Late stage syphilis

After a lull of up to 30 years (the latent stage) the disease may attack any part of the body — notably heart (**h**), blood vessels (**i**), brain (**j**), and spinal cord (**k**). Other effects include mouth ulcers (**l**), and erosion of skin (**m**), bones (**n**) and ligaments (**o**). Major effects can be blindness (**p**), paralysis, insanity and death. Damage is irreversible.

## Congenital syphilis

Mothers with syphilis may pass it to their unborn babies via the placenta. Of babies produced by these mothers, one-third are aborted or born dead (**a**), one-third are born with syphilis (**b**), and one-third are born healthy (**c**). Treatment of the mother early in pregnancy protects the baby, and congenital syphilis is now rare.

©DIAGRAM

# Gonorrhea 1

Gonorrhea is a common infectious disease, with maybe 200 million cases a year worldwide. It is rarely fatal but sometimes has serious complications, mainly in women. The disease organism is a bean-shaped bacterium called *Neisseria gonorrhoeae*. This spreads mainly by direct body contact, usually genital intercourse, with a 50-80% risk of transmission from people already infected. Oral and anal intercourse can also convey gonorrhea. Reputed rare sources of infection include deep kissing, lavatory seats (just possible for some men), and towels or washcloths (with young girls as the victims).

Gonorrhea affects mainly the age group 15-25 years. More men than women show visible signs of infection. These tend to appear after two to ten days' incubation.

Men first notice discharge from the penis and a burning sensation on urinating. Untreated infection can spread through the sexual organs. Fibrous blockage of the urethra may stop a man passing water and inflammation of the testes can make him sterile.

Only 20% of infected women show symptoms or signs of the disease. Then there is vaginal discharge with pain on passing water. The untreated disease can painfully swell glands around the vaginal entrance and invade the womb and beyond with serious results and, rarely, death if peritonitis ensues.

In both sexes long-standing infection invading the bloodstream can affect skin, joints and even brain. Treatment is usually one big dose of penicillin boosted by probenecid. Doses have had to be greatly increased to combat the germ's mounting resistance to antibiotics. Follow-up tests monitor recovery. But a first attack of gonorrhea confers no future immunity.

# Sexual infections

## Gonorrhea in men

Genital infection produces watery (later thicker, greenish-yellow) discharge from the penis (**a**). There is a frequent urge to urinate — an act made burningly painful by inflammation of the urethra (**b**). Fibrous blockage of the urethra can obstruct urine and cause serious damage to the kidneys (**c**). Inflamed epididymides (**d**) produce intense pain and the testes (**e**) may swell as big as apples and cease yielding sperm.

Anal infection (**f**) occurs in homosexuals practicing anal sex. There may be moistness and acute deep pain in the rectum. Mouth infection due to oral-genital sex causes mouth ulcers (**g**) and sore throat (**h**). Long-term widespread infection can produce arthritis (**i**), skin eruptions (**j**), and septicemia with fever (**k**), meningitis (**l**) and heart damage (**m**).

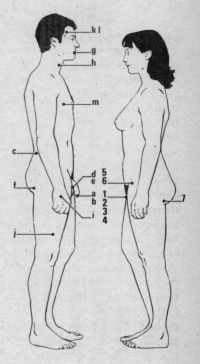

## Gonorrhea in women

Genital infection produces a red, raw vulva (**1**), maybe with unusual — often white, green or yellow — vaginal discharge (**2**). There may be a frequent urge to urinate (**3**) — a scaldingly painful act. Bartholinitis, in which glands (**4**) at the vaginal entrance are inflamed, is a common local complication, as is salpingitis, in which inflamed Fallopian tubes (**5**) give harsh lower-abdominal pain. Abscesses may form in the tubes, ovaries or pelvic cavity (**6**), causing acute colicky pain and menstrual irregularity. Without surgery victims become invalids.

Anal infection (**7**) in a woman can result from anal sex or from her own (infected) vagina. Discharge and bleeding may occur from the rectum.

Effects of mouth infection (**g,h**) and widespread infection (**i-m**) are as in men.

©DIAGRAM

281

# Gonorrhea 2

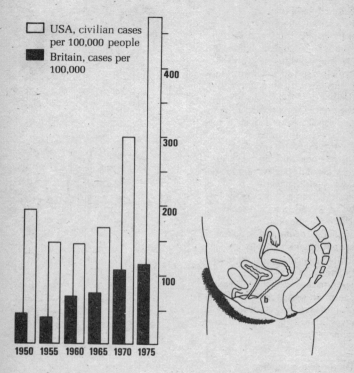

USA, civilian cases per 100,000 people

Britain, cases per 100,000

400

300

200

100

1950 1955 1960 1965 1970 1975

a

b

**Incidence of gonorrhea**
This diagram shows the trend in the USA and Britain. After a post-World War II peak, numbers fell but rose worldwide in the 1960s and 1970s. One reason was the bacterium's evolution into strains with growing resistance to penicillin; by the late '70s one even seemed to thrive on the drug. Then, too, new "symptom-free" strains began to appear.

**Gonorrhea and pregnancy**
Gonorrhea organisms may track up a woman's genital system to block her Fallopian tubes (**a**) and make her sterile for life or cause an ectopic pregnancy with loss of the embryo and often severe illness. At birth babies can get infected eyes from the mother's vagina (**b**). Untreated babies may suffer inflamed eyes and blindness.

# Other notifiable infections

**Other notifiable diseases**
Described here are three other
notifiable sexually transmitted
diseases. The illustration *right*
shows affected areas.

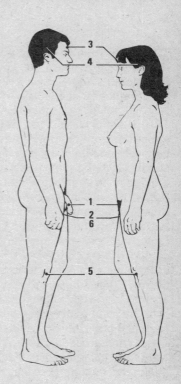

**Granuloma inguinale**
Up to 2 months after infection by
*Donovonia* bacilli, a red painless
papule appears on or by male or
female genitals (**1**). It slowly
spreads, forming bright red
ulcers slow to heal. The scars
often break down, and tissue —
even an entire penis — may be
destroyed. Antibiotic treatment
is used. This disease is rare
outside the tropics.

**Lymphogranuloma venereum**
This mainly tropical disease is
due to a *Chlamydia* bacterium.
Some 5-21 days after infection a
small painless ulcer may show
on the penis or vulva (**1**). Weeks
later painful swellings and
abscesses appear in the groin (**2**).
There may be fever (**3**), headache
(**4**), joint pains (**5**) and genital
swellings (**6**). Treatment is by
antibiotics, and in some late
cases, surgery.

**Chancroid**
This chiefly tropical disease is
also called soft chancre or soft
sore. About 3-7 days after
infection by a *Haemophilus*
bacterium several soft, painful
ulcers appear on male or female
genitals (**1**). Later a painful
one-sided swelling develops in
the groin (**2**) and there are genital
complications. Sulfonamide
drugs usually cure.

©DIAGRAM

# Non-notifiable infections 1

These pages show mostly minor sexually transmitted diseases. They vary in prevalence. Nonspecific genital infections (NSGI) — infections of unidentified origin — are the commonest of all diseases passed on by sexual contact (though not all cases may start in this way).

The usual infection in men is nonspecific urethritis. This is often due to unidentified germs or (where sex is always between the same partners) to the penis reacting to chemicals in the vagina. One to four weeks after intercourse there may be gonorrhea-like symptoms: some discharge from the penis and discomfort on urinating. Untreated infection may involve bladder, testes and prostate, with localized swelling and pain. One per cent of men develop Reiter's disease — a more serious condition with arthritis, conjunctivitis and urethritis.

Conditions commonly occurring among women include nonspecific vaginitis and cervicitis (inflammation of the vagina and cervix), often produced by a change in the kinds of bacteria found in the genital tract. There may be increased vaginal discharge, a frequent urge to urinate, pain on doing so, and abdominal pain.

Antibiotic treatment usually clears up nonspecific infections, though these may recur.

**Incidence of NSGI**
This diagram shows the dramatic increase in the incidence of male nonspecific urethritis in Britain since the mid 1950s. The trend is similar in the USA. Nonspecific cervicitis in women has also become much more common. All figures for NSGI understate the total for not all cases are reported and the condition has no standard definition.

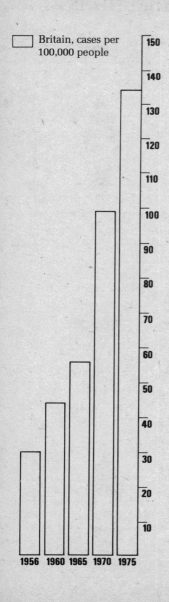

Britain, cases per 100,000 people

150
140
130
120
110
100
90
80
70
60
50
40
30
20
10

1956  1960  1965  1970  1975

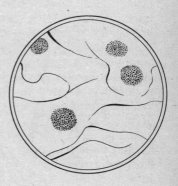

**Chlamydia trachomatis**
This bacterium acts like a virus.
Sometimes it invades the genital
tract. In women it may inflame
the Fallopian tubes and give
sticky eyes to babies about to be
born. In men it can cause
nonspecific urethritis. It may be
to blame for half of all nonspecific
genital infections but goes
undiagnosed for lack of
screening facilities.

©DIAGRAM

285

# Non-notifiable infections 2

### Genital warts
These appear on the genitals or around the anus. Groups form a tiny "cauliflower." They are due to a virus like that giving warts elsewhere on the body and show 1 to 6 months or more after sexual contact. Treatment may be to apply caustic substances, or to freeze or electrically burn. Ordinary warts and syphilitic warts also occur on genitals.

### Molluscum contagiosum
This harmless virus infection can be caught in swimming pools but is usually due to sexual contact. Then it produces small, painless pink spots in the genital area. Smooth and firm, they have a central depression filled with a whitish plug. They appear up to 3 months after contact and last for months. Doctors use caustic substances to remove them.

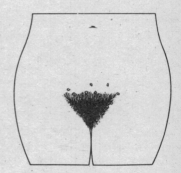

### Genital herpes
This is caused by a similar virus to that producing "cold sores" around the mouth. About 4 or 5 days after sexual contact, itchy blisters appear on the genitals, then burst to produce raw, shallow, painful ulcers. There may be fever and other symptoms. All go in 2 weeks or so, but milder attacks may recur. Cures may now be emerging.

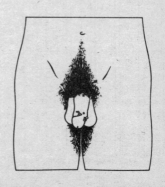

### Trichomoniasis

"Trich" involves a foul-smelling, greenish, foamy vaginal discharge, and inflammation of vagina and vulva with pain on intercourse and perhaps on urination. Most infected men suffer no symptoms but can still spread the disease. Its cause is a microscopic one-celled animal parasite. The cure is an oral course of any of several drugs.

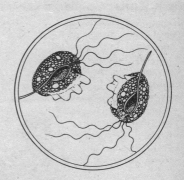

### Candidosis

Also called moniliasis and thrush, in women this can give an itchy swollen vulva; curdy vaginal discharge; and pain on urination and intercourse. Men may have a red, spotty penis and inner foreskin, with a burning feeling. The cause is a yeast-like fungus, treated by fungicidal pessaries in the vagina or creams on the vulva or penis.

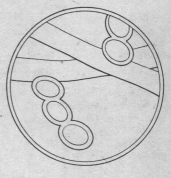

### Infestations

Scabies or "the itch" features small itchy lumps with thin dark lines where tiny scabies mites (**a**) burrow into the skin. The lumps may appear on genitals over a month after infection.

Itching in areas with pubic or other body hair may be due to infestation by crab lice (**b**), sometimes via beds or towels. Infestations are easy to cure.

# Chapter 13

Homosexuals dancing on a New Orleans street corner — an anonymous ink drawing of c. 1890 (Rare Book Room, Tulane University Library, New Orleans).

A WELL KNOWN NUISANCE

# Homosexuals in society 1

Homosexuality, in which a person shows an emotional and physical preference for members of his or her own sex, is as old as history and has occurred in all human societies. In ancient Greece and Rome homosexuality was considered perfectly natural and was widely practiced. Other societies who have accepted it as a normal aspect of sexuality include the Mohave Indians of North America and the Arabs. But by and large most societies have tended to see homosexuality as abnormal — so much so that homosexuals, and male homosexuals in particular, have often been persecuted. Today, even with some liberalization of attitudes and laws,

**San Francisco survey**
Information for the diagrams on this and on subsequent pages are based on the results of a survey of homosexuals living in and around San Francisco, and published in *Homosexualities: A Study of Diversity Among Men and Women* (1978) by Alan P. Bell and Martin S. Weinberg. Their research was backed by The Institute for Sex Research.

**1 Regret about homosexuality**
Shown are percentages of whites in the San Francisco survey who expressed various amounts of regret about their homosexuality. (Of blacks, 59% of males and 73% of females had no regrets.)
a None 49% males, 64% females.
b Very little 24% males, 20% females.
c Some 21% males, 14% females.
d A great deal 6% males, 2% females.

**2 Reasons for regret**
The following percentages are for white males and females only.
**A** Rejection by society
44% males, 46% females.
**B** Cannot have children
32% males, 24% females.
**C** Reduced life options
15% males, 18% females.
**D** Feelings of loneliness
14% males, 8% females.
**E** Other 44% males, 49% females.
■ Males ☐ Females

homosexuality or homosexual acts still continue to be illegal or discriminated against in many parts of the world. As a result, homosexuals are still prey to difficult personal and social problems. Initially many homosexuals have difficulty in admitting their sexual preference even to themselves — on average it takes about six years for a homosexual to "come out." Often there are problems at work or in other situations, caused largely by fear of exposure and its possible consequences. Even with the new "gay" militancy, many homosexuals tend to suppress natural expressions of their sexuality such as flirting, and

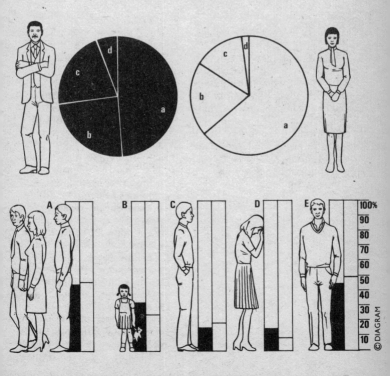

# Homosexuals in society 2

some may even feel a need to play a token part in heterosexual relations. Also, despite the emergence of a gay subculture in some large cities, social isolation and loneliness can be serious problems.

Although many theories have been put forward to explain homosexuality, most have been greatly oversimplified and based largely on research into homosexuals who have sought psychiatric help. Two physical-cause theories are that homosexuality is an inherited genetic tendency, or that it is the result of an imbalance of the sex hormones. Findings for both these theories, however, have been ambiguous and

**Overtness**

Here we compare the overtness of white male and female homosexuals in the San Francisco survey. More females than males thought that parents and heterosexual friends knew about their homosexuality, but more males than females believed their homosexuality was known to employers, fellow workers and neighbors. Trends among black homosexuals were broadly similar.

**1 Father (if living)**
a Neither knows nor suspects 53% males, 46% females.
b Suspects 16% (m), 17% (f).
c Knows 31% (m), 37% (f).

**2 Mother (if living)**
a Neither knows nor suspects 38% males, 32% females.
b Suspects 21% (m), 19% (f).
c Knows 42% (m), 49% (f).

**3 Employer**
a Neither knows nor suspects 53% males, 68% females.
b Suspects 18% (m), 17% (f).
c Knows 29% (m), 15% (f).

**4 Heterosexual friends**
a None know 21% (m), 16% (f).
b Few know 27% (m), 30% (f).
c Most know 29% (m), 39% (f).

**5 Fellow workers**
a None know 31% (m), 48% (f).
b Few know 31% (m), 28% (f).
c Most know 29% (m), 15% (f).

**6 Neighbors**
a None know 49% (m), 63% (f).
b Few know 28% (m), 21% (f).
c Most know 14% (m), 11% (f).
■ Males    □ Females

contradictory. A third, and possibly more convincing theory, is that all people have a potential for homosexuality and that certain experiences in childhood or adolescence, particularly within the family, have the effect of reinforcing this natural potential.

More constructive than searching for "causes" or "cures" for homosexuality are current attempts to encourage greater public understanding of this form of sexuality. For only when the many myths surrounding homosexuality have been finally destroyed can today's homosexuals hope to win general acceptance of their "right to be gay."

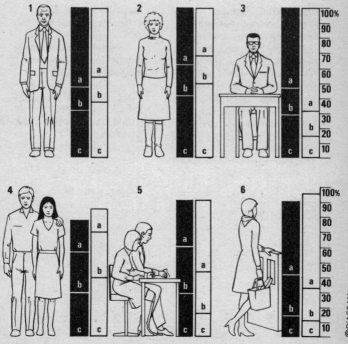

# Homosexual activity 1

There are a great many myths about homosexuals and about homosexual lovemaking in particular. Among the most persistent of these myths is the idea that homosexuals, and particularly male homosexuals, are primarily sexual creatures, constantly engaged in the hunt for sexual partners, incapable of forming a profound alliance, and considerably more promiscuous than their heterosexual counterparts. In fact — although some would claim that it is not strictly relevant to compare homosexual with heterosexual activity — it would appear that homosexuals are typically no more or no less active than heterosexuals.

**Homosexual practices**
Here we compare the favorite lovemaking activities of male and female homosexuals taking part in the San Francisco survey. Percentages are based on the replies of 552 white and 108 black homosexual males, and of 210 white and 59 black homosexual females.
Oral-genital sex was very popular with homosexuals of both sexes. Anal intercourse, though enjoyed by many white male homosexuals, was especially popular with blacks.

**Favorites among males**
1 Performing anal intercourse 26% whites, 44% blacks.
2 Receiving oral-genital sex 27% whites, 18% blacks.
3 Mutual oral-genital sex 14% whites, 8% blacks.
4 Receiving anal intercourse 5% whites, 11% blacks.
5 Self masturbation 5% whites, 3% blacks.

**Favorites among females**
6 Receiving oral-genital sex 20% whites, 29% blacks.
7 Mutual oral-genital sex 20% whites, 24% blacks.
8 Body rubbing (tribadism) 12% whites, 24% blacks.
9 Being masturbated by partner 16% whites, 5% blacks.
10 Mutual masturbation 13% whites, 7% blacks.

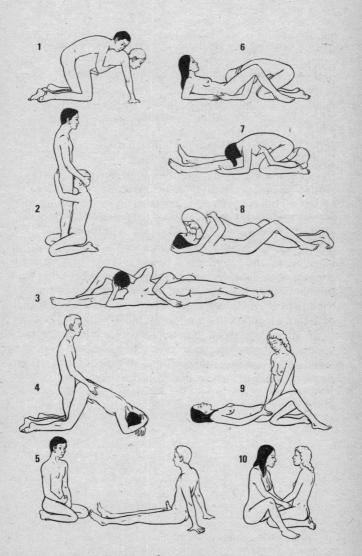

# Homosexual activity 2

Nor do homosexual relationships conform to a particular stereotype; the emotional and physical aspects of homosexual relationships are just as diverse as they are among heterosexual couples.

Another common misconception is that each partner within a homosexual relationship adopts an exclusively active ("butch") or exclusively passive ("femme") role. In practice, active and passive roles are interchangeable and if adopted at all by a couple are often alternated.

In terms of lovemaking activities, with the exception of penile-vaginal penetration, there are many similarities between homosexual and heterosexual practices. Activities among male and female homosexuals include kissing, petting, caressing, oral-genital contact, and mutual masturbation. Exclusive to males are fellatio, anal intercourse, and interfemoral coitus in which one partner's penis is stimulated by being moved between the other's thighs. Among lesbians cunnilungus is common, as is tribadism in which one partner lies on top of the other and both move together to stimulate the other's clitoris. Contrary to the image presented in much hard-core pornography, very few lesbians have ever used a dildo; lesbian lovemaking centers around clitoral stimulation and so has no need of penile penetration or penis substitutes.

# Homosexuality

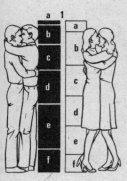

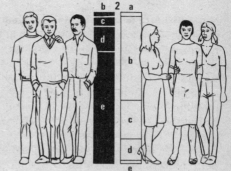

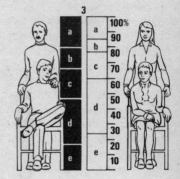

## 1 Activity in past year

White males in the San Francisco survey reported higher levels of homosexual activity than those reported by white females.

**a** None 3% males, 8% females.
**b** Once a month or less 13% males, 21% females.
**c** 2-3 times a month 17% males, 20% females.
**d** Once a week 22% males, 20% females.
**e** 2-3 times a week 30% males, 19% females.
**f** 4 or more times a week 17% males, 13% females.

## 2 Number of partners ever

White males reported many more partners than white females.

**a** 1 partner 0% (m), 3% (f).
**b** 2-9: 3% (m), 55% (f).
**c** 10-24: 6% (m), 26% (f).
**d** 25-99: 17% (m), 13% (f).
**e** 100+: 75% (m), 2% (f).

## 3 Living arrangement

White homosexuals currently living with their partner viewed the arrangement as follows.

**a** Not important 20% (m), 14% (f).
**b** Nice but not important 13% (m), 8% (f).
**c** Somewhat important 20% (m), 17% (f).
**d** Very important 30% (m), 35% (f).
**e** Most important thing in life 17% (m), 24% (f).

■ Males
□ Females

©DIAGRAM

297

# Bisexuality 1

Exclusive heterosexuality and exclusive homosexuality can be seen as the two extremes of the human sexual spectrum. For in addition to persons whose psychosexual responses and overt sexual activity are directed exclusively toward members of one sex or the other, there is another group whose sexual interest or activity may be termed "bisexual," being directed at members of both sexes.

Some people combine approximately equal amounts of heterosexual and homosexual activity during all periods of their sexually active lives. Others may appear to be exclusively heterosexual in one period and exclusively homosexual in another. Yet others are predominantly heterosexual or predominantly homosexual all through their lives, but show varying degrees of sexual involvement with persons not of their preferred sex.

# Homosexuality

## Kinsey ratings

Summarized here is Kinsey's scale for measuring the entire heterosexual-homosexual range.

**0:** Exclusively heterosexual, all psychosexual responses and all overt sexual activity directed toward opposite sex.

**1:** Responses and activity almost entirely heterosexual, but with incidental homosexual responses or activity.

**2:** Psychosexual responses and/or overt sexual activity mainly heterosexual, but responses to homosexual stimuli rather definite and/or homosexual activity more than incidental.

**3:** At the middle of the scale, about equally heterosexual and homosexual in psychosexual responses and/or overt activity.

**4:** Responses and activity more often homosexual, but responses to heterosexual stimuli rather definite and/or heterosexual activity more than incidental.

**5:** Responses and activity almost entirely homosexual, but with incidental heterosexual responses and/or activity.

**6:** Exclusively homosexual, all psychosexual responses and all overt sexual activity directed toward people of same sex.

# Bisexuality 2

It is extremely difficult to estimate the number of bisexuals in a population, for bisexuals are subject to the same sort of social discrimination as persons who are exclusively homosexual. Research by Alfred Kinsey in the 1940s, however, suggested that more than one third of all men and nearly one fifth of all women have at least one homosexual experience to orgasm.

**San Francisco study**
This diagram shows percentages of white males and white females taking part in the San Francisco Bay Area study of homosexuals who were given various ratings according to the Kinsey scale of heterosexuality-homosexuality.
**6:** 74% males, 68% females.
**5:** 18% males, 19% females.
**4:** 3% males, 5% females.
**1-3:** 5% males, 8% females.

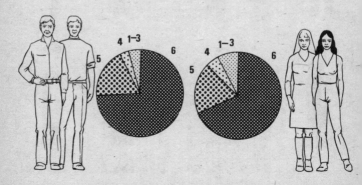

# Homosexuality

## On the Kinsey scale
This diagram shows percentages of 25-year-old single and married males and females in Kinsey's surveys who were given different heterosexual-homosexual ratings. Females in the survey were high school and college educated; for males we include here the percentages for high-school educated whites.

**A) Single males**
Only 51% were rated exclusively heterosexual, while a total of 31% were rated predominantly or exclusively homosexual.

**B) Married males**
92% were rated heterosexual only; the others were rated 1-3.

**C) Single females**
Compared to single males, many more of this group were at the heterosexual end of the scale (84% rated 0, 5% rated 1).

**D) Married females**
Here the pattern was similar to that for married males (92% rated 0, 7% rated 1 or 2).

# Chapter 14

An engraving by Pieter
Bruegel the Elder (c. 1525-1569)
on the theme of sexual excess.

# Unconventional sex

LVXVRIA

VIRES, EFFOEMINAT ARTVS.

# Swinging 1

There is nothing new about group sex or mate swapping. The Ancient Greeks and Romans indulged in fairly wild orgies, while the Eskimos are renowned for their tradition of offering their wives as a gesture of hospitality to visiting travelers. But the modern phenomenon of organized "wife swapping" or "swinging" is comparatively new.

Swinging — where one established couple swaps partners with at least one other established couple — first aroused public interest in the United States in the late 1950s. Since then it has received considerable media coverage and has become a common feature of much soft and hard core pornography. No one knows just how widespread swinging is, and its incidence has possibly been exaggerated. But it certainly occurs in the United States, Britain and some other European countries. Research suggests that it is commonest among white, fairly affluent, middle class couples in their late twenties or early thirties who have perhaps become bored with their marriages or established sexual relationships.

Swinging takes various forms — the two most common being the foursome and the party. The foursome involves two heterosexual couples who swap partners either in a "closed" fashion, where the two swapped couples separate, engage in sexual intercourse, and then meet up again, or in an "open" fashion, where both couples participate in sexual activity together as a sexual foursome, often also including lovemaking between the two women. Lovemaking between the two men is less common.

Parties, which may also be "closed" or "open," are usually held in a private home and any number of couples may be invited. The "closed" party usually follows an established routine and sexual activity between couples occurs in private, away from the rest of the party. By contrast, sexual activity at an "open" party is openly displayed and viewed, perhaps with up to 10 or 12 people participating in sex together as a group.

In some countries the swinging scene is highly organized and ritualized. In the United States, for example, there are swinging magazines, newspapers, clubs, societies and bars. There is also a swingers' terminology. Except among other participants, swingers do not generally publicly admit to their activities. Instead, swingers usually find other similarly minded couples through carefully phrased advertisements in magazines or newspapers or at recognized clubs or bars. Interested newcomers to the scene are typically recruited or seduced by established swingers.

# Swinging 2

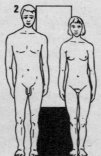
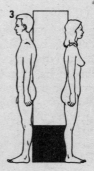

**Marital status** (*above*)
In some areas unmarried people are largely excluded from the swinging scene, but, as this diagram demonstrates, J.R. and L.G. Smith found that fairly high percentages of their San Francisco sample were either single or formerly married.
1 Married 44%.
2 Single 32%.
3 Formerly married 24%.

**Average age** (*below*)
This diagram shows the age characteristics of a sample of 503 active mate-swappers in the San Francisco Bay Area (J.R. and L.G. Smith, 1970). Of those studied, 89% were aged between 21 and 50, whereas only 4% were under 21 and 7% over 50. The average age for women in the sample was 28 (**A**) and for men 34 (**B**).

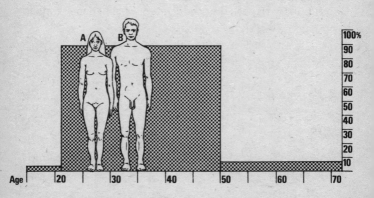

# Unconventional sex

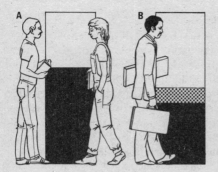

**Education and occupation** (*above*)
Among mate-swappers in the
San Francisco survey (Smith,
1970), 52% were college
graduates and a further 12% were
still students (**A**). Another survey
of American swingers (G.D.
Bartell, 1974) looked at the
occupations of people taking
part: 40-50% of the men were
salesmen (**B**), and 90% of the
women were full-time
housewives (**C**).

**Number of partners** (*below*)
According to the San Francisco
survey, mate-swappers typically
have many rather than a few
other partners: 23% of the men
and 12% of the women claimed
to have had more than 100
partners. Our diagram shows the
median number of partners
claimed by respondents: for men
(**1**) the median was 19 and for
women (**2**) it was 15.

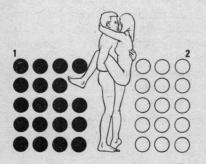

● Men's other partners

○ Women's other partners

# Sadomasochism

Sadism — named for the Marquis de Sade (1740-1814) — is the term used to describe the sexual pleasure or excitement gained by inflicting pain on a partner. Masochism — named for another infamous writer about sexual exploits, Leopold von Sacher-Masoch (1836-1895) — describes the wish to receive pain and the obtaining of sexual pleasure through being hurt or humiliated. Sadomasochism is a sexual variance characterized by extreme domination and submissiveness and by the giving and receiving of pain as techniques of sexual activity. It is so-called because all practitioners have both a sadistic and a masochistic side to their personalities, although one or the other is dominant. To a limited extent all couples demonstrate some degree of sadomasochism. Pain in the form of love bites or scratching is a normal part of many couples' lovemaking, while within a relationship one partner is usually more dominant than the other. The behavior patterns of true sadomasochists, however, are considerably more complex. Activities may include beating with the hand or with various implements, pinching, biting or even burning. A partner may also be tied up, gagged, blindfolded or otherwise immobilized. Pain or humiliation may also be inflicted verbally. Usually the couple follows a fairly elaborate and planned "sex game" in which one partner has supposedly done something wrong for which he or she must be punished. At the same time, within most sadomasochistic partnerships, very strict "rules" are observed so that the amount of pain inflicted is only as much as the submissive partner enjoys or is prepared to accept.

Although to most people sadomasochistic activities seem to be inexplicably cruel, it does appear that pain or thoughts of pain can be extremely powerful sources of sexual arousal. Certainly sadomasochism is a favorite theme in both hard and soft pornography.

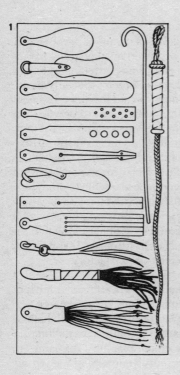

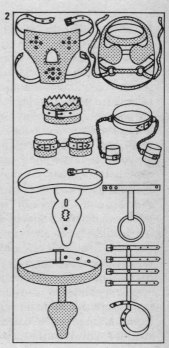

**Special equipment**
Equipment for sadomasochists
falls into two broad categories; a
few examples are shown here.
**1** Flagellation implements,
including paddles, canes, straps
and tawse as well as whips.
**2** Bondage items, including
masks, collars, handcuffs, ankle
cuffs, harnesses, chastity belts, as
well as straps and rings for penis
and testes.

©DIAGRAM

# Fetishism

Fetishism, like sadomasochism, is a common pornographic theme and is found to some degree in most people's sex lives. A person may be aroused by one particular body part, such as breasts, buttocks or legs, and men especially may derive considerable stimulation from an inanimate object such as an item of underclothing. But for most people these are just stimuli; they may form the basis for fantasies or they may enhance lovemaking but they are not a substitute for more conventional sexual activity. For the true fetishist, however, they become the sole object of his sexual attention. Strictly the fetishist is someone who is unable to enjoy sex without the presence of a fetish. In extreme cases it may even become a substitute for a real human partner. Usually fetishism derives from childhood experiences in which the fetish object is somehow associated with sexual excitement; later this fixation is reinforced by unsatisfactory interpersonal relationships.

Exotic garments in rubber, leather or vinyl are now fairly openly available in many countries and have to a large extent replaced more traditional fetish objects. Fetishists either use them for solo dressing sessions or may share sessions with a similarly fixated partner.

## Fetish objects

Traditionally the fetishist centered his or her attention on a particular body part such as hair, ears, breasts or feet (**1**), and sometimes on particular fabrics or items of clothing such as leather, rubber, fur, boots, corsets or rainwear (**2**). Many now prefer specialist garments widely available in leather, rubber and vinyl (**3**).

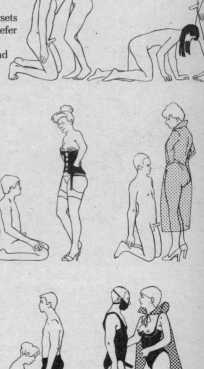

**1**

**2**

**3**

©DIAGRAM

# Transvestism

Transvestism, or cross-dressing, is a sexual activity in which emotional and physical pleasure are derived from dressing in the clothes of the opposite sex. Most transvestites are men. Women, of course, may dress in masculine clothes without seeming in any way abnormal. Like most variant sexual behavior, transvestism is surrounded by misconceptions. Most common is the idea that all transvestites are homosexual. In fact, probably not more than 25% of transvestites are overtly homosexual. Most are heterosexual with fairly conventional sex lives, and many are married with children. Cross-dressing is their only variant sexual activity. Also contrary to popular belief, the true transvestite has no wish to change sex physically — only to cross-dress. Patterns of cross-dressing vary. Transvestites may cross-dress occasionally or frequently, or may reject male clothing completely to masquerade all the time as a female. Sometimes there is a more fetish-like approach, perhaps involving a single garment. Concern over the perfect fit of clothing may be obsessional. Removing clothing may be as important a ritual as putting it on. Many transvestites gain sexual pleasure from masturbating while looking at a self-reflection in a mirror. Transvestism is a complex phenomenon and what is known about it has been learned mainly from transvestites who have sought help. Cross-dressing tends to be a secret activity, sometimes begun in early childhood, perhaps as a result of parental rejection of the child's sex. Some transvestites develop a form of dual personality — one male and one female — and cross-dressing becomes a way of expressing the female part while remaining fundamentally masculine. To many transvestites cross-dressing brings relaxation, relief and a sense of safety. They are freed from the demands of the male role, and the outer layer of "femininity" assures them that their violent feelings are safely contained.

# Unconventional sex

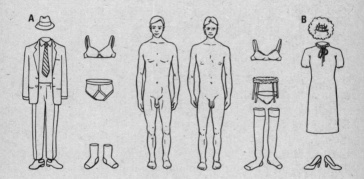

## Cross-dressing

Patterns of cross-dressing vary.
Some transvestites like always to
wear a particular item of
clothing, such as a brassiere,
under their normal everyday
clothing (**A**). Others prefer to
wear an entire outfit of female
clothing, perhaps with a female
wig (**B**); cross-dressing of this
type ranges in frequency from
occasional to continual.

©DIAGRAM

313

# Transsexualism

Transsexualism, also known as sex role inversion, is an extremely complex situation in which an individual believes that he or she has been given a body of the wrong sex. Whereas the transvestite is satisfied merely to dress in the clothing of the opposite sex, the transsexual seeks a much more fundamental change — a physical change of sex to bring what is considered to be an inappropriate body into line with his or her own gender identity.

Like transvestism, transsexualism occurs mainly in men. There are, however, reports of a very few female to male transsexuals; male hormones are taken to deepen the voice and to increase the body hair, making a full beard a possibility, and as with men surgery is possible to reconstruct the genitals. Allowing for these very rare exceptions, transsexualism is an essentially male phenomenon and it is on men that we concentrate here. The male transsexual is a person whose anatomy and genetic make-up are completely male. He has normal male genitals and is physically capable of having intercourse with a woman. But in every way he rejects his maleness, perhaps coming to hate his sex organs so much that self-castration or suicide may be attempted. In every way — emotional, physical and sexual — the male transsexual wants to be a woman and, as a woman, to have a heterosexual relationship with a man.

Although transsexuals may obtain some relief from cross-dressing, they are primarily concerned with obtaining a surgical sex-change. Out of an estimated 10,000 transsexuals in the United States, between 3000 and 4000 have now had sex-reassignment operations. Such operations are carried out in the United States and Europe only after detailed investigation of each case, and costs can be high. A recent victory won by US transsexuals is the right to marry following a sex-reassignment operation; this right is still denied to transsexuals in the United Kingdom.

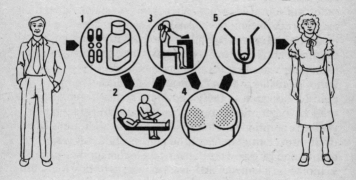

**Male to female sex change**
We show the typical pattern. The
first three are preconditions of a
legal sex change operation.
1 Taking female hormones.
2 Psychiatric counseling.
3 Living full-time as a female,
usually for at least one year.
4 Breasts may be surgically
augmented with silicone pads.
5 Sex change operation in which
the genitals are remodeled.

© DIAGRAM

315

# Exhibitionism

Exhibitionism is a sexual variance in which a person, usually a man, obtains sexual pleasure and gratification from exposing his sex organs to an unsuspecting person, usually a woman or perhaps a child. Most women at some time or another are confronted by an exhibitionist. The encounter may take place almost anywhere: in the street, in a park, or on a bus or train.

Although exhibitionism is classed as a crime (also see Chapter 15), exhibitionists are generally thought to be more of a nuisance than a menace. Exhibitionists do not often become involved in more serious crime, and if they do their offenses are usually nonsexual. The typical exhibitionist is a quiet and submissive man whose aim is to shock rather than to hurt or to initiate any form of sexual participation. Gratification comes from the other person's reaction, which is wrongly believed to express sexual excitement. Later, this forms the basis for masturbatory fantasies.

Exhibitionists range in age from young adolescent to elderly. Research suggests, however, that all have an inadequate or immature approach to sexuality combined with a profound need to be noticed. Often they come from a puritanical family background, and as children were dominated by a powerful, over-possessive mother. Many exhibitionists are married, leading very ordinary lives, but their sexual relationships tend to be poor and their frequency of intercourse low. Exhibitionism provides them with an opportunity to demonstrate their virility without the threat of a deeper sexual and human involvement. For some, genital exposure is a rare or one-off occurrence. For others it is more compulsive, with incidents frequently occurring at the same location and at the same time of day. It appears that many have a secret wish to be caught and punished. Psychiatric counseling can be very helpful.

### Exhibitionism
Sexual gratification for the exhibitionist comes from other people's shocked reactions to the sight of his genitals (**1**). Mistakenly believing that their reaction was one of sexual excitement, the exhibitionist later remembers the incident and uses it as a basis for masturbatory fantasies (**2**).

# Voyeurism

Definitions of voyeurism vary, but for our purposes we shall take it to mean the gaining of unusual sexual pleasure and gratification through the surreptitious observation of naked persons or sexual acts. Like the exhibitionist, the compulsive voyeur, or "peeper," is liable to prosecution (also see Chapter 15). But whereas the activity of the exhibitionist is necessarily carried out in the open, the illicit character of peeping makes detection less likely. The typical voyeur, whose aim is solely to peep, is generally considered to be more of a nuisance than a danger, but in some cases peeping is combined with other crimes such as burglary, arson or rape.

Almost everyone derives pleasure from looking at a physically attractive member of the opposite sex, and many ordinary couples add to their sexual enjoyment by watching themselves in a mirror during lovemaking. The compulsive voyeur, however, differs from the normal in several important respects. Firstly, he goes to quite considerable lengths to observe others when he has no right to do so and when his presence is unlikely to be detected. Secondly, the act of observation is usually, although not always, an end in itself. The typical "Peeping Tom" is a timid and frightened individual who is unlikely to wish for or to attempt sexual assault. He has no desire to initiate sexual involvement but instead gets gratification simply from the act of looking and from the fact that his activity is forbidden. By just looking the voyeur is able to maintain a feeling of sexual superiority without running any risk of failure or rejection by a real partner.

**Voyeurism and scoptophilia**
Strictly speaking, voyeurism refers only to the gaining of unusual sexual gratification from watching nudes (**A**). In practice, however, this term is also often applied to what is more correctly known as scoptophilia: the derivation of sexual pleasure from observing genitals or sexual acts (**B**).

# Chapter 15

The Romans walking off with *the Sabine Women* — a none too serious book illustration by the 19th century English caricaturist John Leech.

# Sexual offenses 1

Sex crime is an extremely emotive subject, involving
important issues of public and personal morality. The extent
to which the sexual activities of consenting adults should be
regulated by law remains a matter for debate, although
recent years have seen a fairly general tendency toward
greater liberality in this respect. Few people now believe
that activities such as non-coital lovemaking or extramarital
sex should be treated as crimes, and for this reason they are
not discussed in detail in this chapter. However, two major
issues that also involve consensual sexual activity —
prostitution (pp. 326-327) and homosexuality (pp. 328-329) –
have been picked out for more detailed scrutiny in relation
to the law. Greater liberality is also evident in the treatment
of "public nuisance" offenders such as exhibitionists or
peepers (pp. 336-337), although few people would like to see
offenses of this type actually excluded from the law. Even
fewer people would argue against the need for the legal
protection of children and minors from sexual advances by
adults (pp. 334-335). Forcible rape, too, is generally
condemned as a serious and reprehensible crime (pp. 330-333)
although the severity of penalties enforced varies a great
deal from one jurisdiction to another.

**Percentage of total crime**
As this diagram based on 1978
official US crime statistics shows,
arrests for sex offenses make up
only a tiny proportion (2%) of
total arrests. Large numbers of
sex offenses, however, are
believed to go unreported —
sometimes because of mutual
consent, and sometimes because
victims are reluctant to be
involved in a sex case.

# Sex and crime

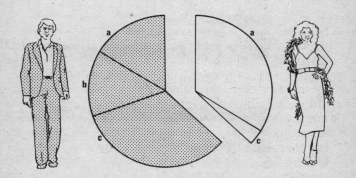

**Types of offense** (*above*)
This diagram, based on official US crime statistics for 1978, breaks down the total number of sex offense arrests according to gender (men 63%, women 37%) and also into three offense types.
**a** Prostitution/commercial vice: 50% (16% men, 34% women).
**b** Forcible rape: 14% (men only).
**c** Other sex offenses: 36% (33% men, 3% women).

**Age of offenders** (*below*)
Also based on official US crime statistics for 1978, this diagram shows an age breakdown of persons of both sexes charged with sexual offenses. The largest group (45% of the total) were aged 18-24 years. A further 37% were aged 25-44 years. Contradicting the "dirty old man" theory, only 3% were over 55 years old.

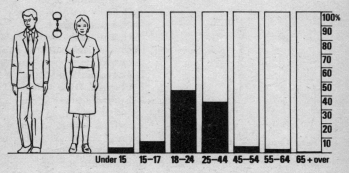

# Sexual offenses 2

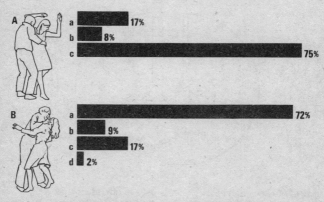

**Relationship of offenders** (*above*)
This diagram, based on a study of the offenses of imprisoned sex offenders (Gebhard et al: 1965), shows offender to adult victim relationships in two types of offense: heterosexual offenses without force or threats (**A**), and heterosexual aggressions (**B**). Relationships were: stranger (**a**), acquaintance (**b**), friend (**c**), relative (**d**).

**Location of offenses** (*right*)
This diagram provides a comparison of common and less common locations for different types of sex offense. Like the preceding diagram, it is based on a US study of offenses by imprisoned sex offenders (P. Gebhard, J. Gagnon, W. Pomeroy, C. Christenson *Sex Offenders: An Analysis of Types*, 1965). Offenses were grouped under the following headings.
**A** Heterosexual offenses (no force or threats used).
**B** Heterosexual aggressions (force and threats used).
**C** Incest offenses.
**D** Homosexual offenses.
**E** Peeping.
**F** Exhibitionism.

**A**
- Residence 56%
- Outdoors 15%
- Automobile 13%
- Theater 9%
- School 1%
- Other 5%

**B**
- Residence 27%
- Outdoors 37%
- Automobile 28%
- Public toilet 3%
- Other 5%

**C**
- Residence 93%
- Outdoors 3%
- Automobile 3%
- School 1%

**D**
- Residence 37%
- Outdoors 21%
- Automobile 14%
- Theater 5%
- Public toilet 12%
- School 1%
- Other 9%

**E**
- Residence 4%
- Outdoors 94%
- School 1%

**F**
- Residence 11%
- Outdoors 57%
- Automobile 19%
- Theater 2%
- Public toilet 1%
- School 2%
- Other 7%

**Key**
- Residence
- Outdoors
- Automobile
- Theater
- Public toilet
- School
- Other

© DIAGRAM

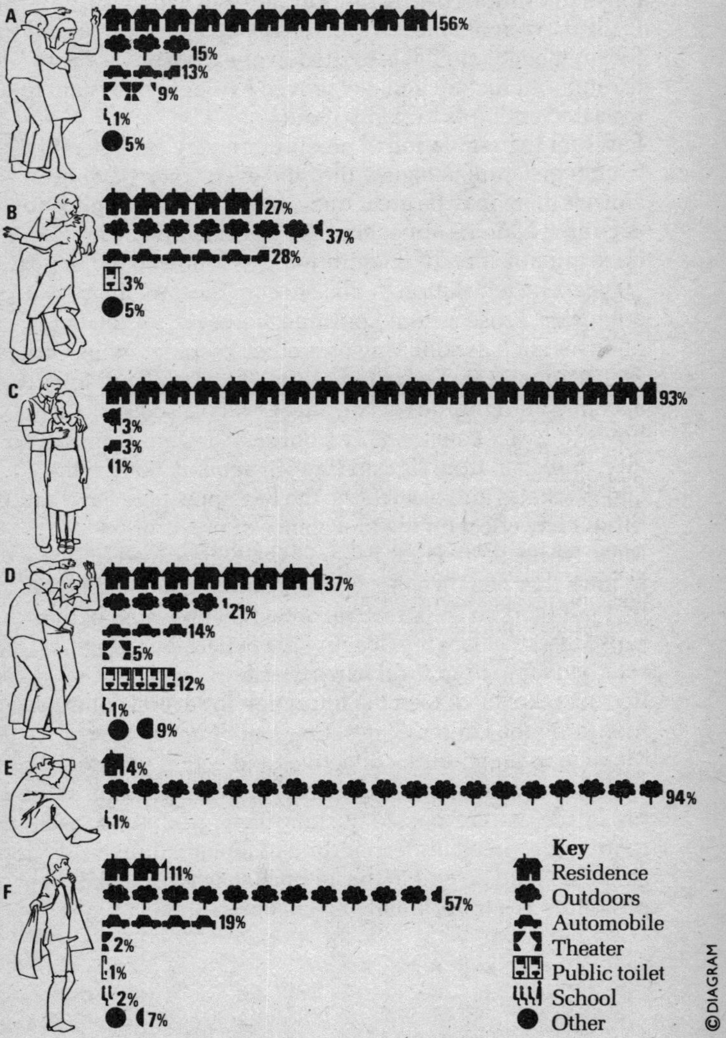

# Prostitution

Legal definitions of prostitution vary, but generally the term is used to refer to indiscriminate sexual activity engaged in for financial gain. It has existed in one form or another throughout history and has proved extremely resistant to repeated attempts to stamp it out.

Laws for the regulation of prostitution vary considerably from legislature to legislature, and even where laws are similar there may be great unevenness in their application. A United Nations appeal in 1949 for the universal decriminalization of prostitution was followed in the next 10 years by legislation to this effect in most member countries. Prosecutions continue, however, for related offenses such as soliciting or brothel-keeping. In the United States, prostitution continues to be illegal in all jurisdictions except some counties of Nevada. Levels of prosecution, however, vary considerably from state to state, from city to city, and even from time to time. In general, both in the United States and elsewhere, the law appears to have had little if any effect on the prevalence of prostitution. Meanwhile, there would seem to be widespread injustice in laws that penalize the prostitute but not her clients, or that fall hard on the streetwalker at the lower end of the prostitutes' scale while leaving the expensive call-girl relatively free from legal harassment.

Recent years have seen the formation in several countries, including the United States, England, France, Japan and Mexico, of prostitutes' collectives and action groups. In addition to seeking an improvement in the position of the prostitute with respect to the law, these groups also seek more widespread understanding of the prostitute's position in society and an end to the ambivalence with which the prostitute has traditionally been viewed.

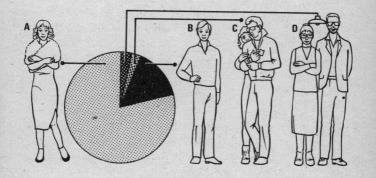

**Related offenses**

Even where prostitution is itself legal, prosecutions continue for related offenses. This diagram shows a breakdown for England and Wales of convictions related to prostitution in 1978.

**A** Female soliciting 80%.
**B** Male soliciting 15%.
**C** Male living on a female prostitute's earnings 3%.
**D** Brothel-keeping 2%.

©DIAGRAM

327

# Homosexual offenses

Homosexuals almost everywhere continue to be subjected to considerable degrees of legal harassment and prosecution. Although homosexuality as such is generally not illegal, some legislatures continue to treat all homosexual acts as crimes, even those between consenting adults in private. A more tolerant attitude has resulted elsewhere in the legalization of consensual homosexual activity in private, but even then, homosexuals frequently find themselves liable to prosecution. Traveling to another country or another state may result in confusion over the legal age of consent, which is in some places higher than the corresponding age for heterosexual relations. Another area of difficulty is the definition of what constitutes a private or a public place. Most often, arrests of homosexuals are for soliciting or for overt sexual activity in public or semipublic places. Homosexuals must exercise extreme caution before making displays of sexuality that would cause no trouble at all if made between heterosexuals. Other crimes involving homosexuals are equivalents of heterosexual offenses: prostitution and homosexual rape. In addition, and despite greater social understanding of homosexuality, homosexuals continue to be victims of alarming degrees of blackmail, robbery and even murder.

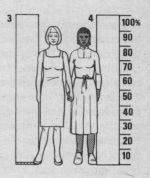

**Homosexual convictions** (*above*)
This diagram, based on a survey of San Francisco homosexuals (see p. 290), shows percentages of homosexuals with one or more convictions related to their homosexuality. Convictions were much commoner among males.
1 White males 15%.
2 Black males 7%.
3 White females 1%.
4 Black females 0%.

**Robbed or rolled** (*below*)
The San Francisco survey also asked homosexuals whether they had ever been robbed or rolled in connection with their homosexuality. As this diagram shows, fairly high percentages of males had been victims.
A White males 38%.
B Black males 21%.
C White females 2%.
D Black females 5%.

©DIAGRAM

329

# Rape 1

The forcing of sexual intercourse upon an unwilling victim
is one of the most serious of all sex crimes. Officially termed
"forcible rape" in the United States (to differentiate it from
"statutory rape," see page 335) it is a violent and hostile
crime which through its total violation of personal and
physical privacy can have a devastating effect on the victim.
The last twenty years have seen a dramatic increase in
forcible rape cases in the United States and elsewhere. From
1960 to 1978 the annual rate of reported rapes in the United
States increased from 9.6 to 30.8 per 100,000 inhabitants.
Any change in the actual incidence of rape itself
must remain a matter of conjecture: there is no way of
measuring the extent to which the increase in reported rapes
results from a greater willingness among victims to report
that they have been raped. Even today, rape remains one of
the most unreported of all crimes.

Young girls and women under the age of twenty-five are the
most likely rape victims; rapists, too, tend to be young.
Contrary to popular belief, rapist and victim are almost
always of the same race, and more often than not the rapist is
someone who is known or at least recognized by the victim.
Many rapes occur in or near the victim's home, often during
the daytime. Despite the common myth that women who are
raped must in some way have "asked for it," research
suggests that in fewer than five per cent of cases can women
be said to have encouraged the attack either by their
appearance or behavior. One study showed that over
seventy per cent of rapes were premeditated.

Although the courts today are more sympathetic to rape
victims than they were, it is still difficult for a woman to win
a rape case. Victims are recommended to seek the help of a
rape victim support group. Penalties for convicted rapists
range in the United States from a short prison term to life
imprisonment or even death.

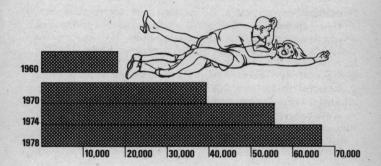

| | | | | | | |
|---|---|---|---|---|---|---|
| 1960 | | | | | | |
| 1970 | | | | | | |
| 1974 | | | | | | |
| 1978 | | | | | | |
| 10,000 | 20,000 | 30,000 | 40,000 | 50,000 | 60,000 | 70,000 |

**Reported rapes**
This diagram, based on official
US figures, shows a dramatic
increase in the number of
reported rapes: the 1978 figure is
almost four times that for 1960.
The extent to which the crime
itself is increasing is unclear;
support centers for victims and
changing social attitudes now
make it easier for a woman to
report a rape.

© DIAGRAM

# Rape 2

Completed rapes

Attempted rapes

**Percentages reported** (*above*)
This diagram, based on a study (M.J. Hindelang and Bruce L. Davis) of rape victims in selected US cities, shows percentages of victims who reported completed or attempted rapes to the police. Whites (**1**) were apparently more reluctant to report rapes than were blacks or other races (**2**). (Other writers have suggested very much lower reporting rates.)

**Reasons for not reporting** (*below*)
Also based on the Hindelang and Davis study, this diagram shows percentages of whites (**1**) and blacks and others (**2**) who gave various reasons for not reporting completed rapes.
**a** Private matter.
**b** Did not want to get involved.
**c** Fear of reprisals.
**d** Lack of proof.
**e** Did not want to bother police.

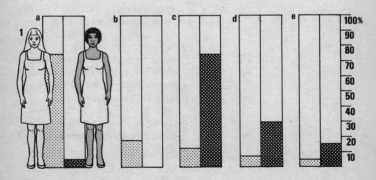

# Sex and crime

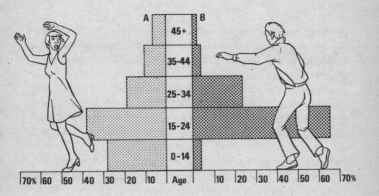

Age scale:
70% 60 50 40 30 20 10 | Age | 10 20 30 40 50 60 70%

Age groups (top to bottom): 45+, 35-44, 25-34, 15-24, 0-14

A | B

**Age of victims and rapists** (*above*)
This diagram, based on another US rape study (M. Amir *Patterns of Forcible Rape*), shows percentages of rape victims (**A**) and rapists (**B**) in different age groups. Among rape victims, 28% were aged 14 years or under, and 38% were aged 15-24 years. Of rapists in the study, 66% were aged 15-24 years, and 24% were aged 25-34 years.

**Use of violence** (*below*)
Beating was involved in nearly half the rapes studied by Amir; other victims suffered choking and "roughness." In nonviolent cases victims had been shown weapons or threatened verbally.
**a** No physical force 15%.
**b** Roughness 28%.
**c** Beaten 25%.
**d** Beaten brutally 21%.
**e** Choked 11%.

© DIAGRAM

# Offenses against children

Persons committing sex offenses against children or minors are among the most feared and hated of all sex offenders. Whether or not the severity of public reaction is always justified is a subject for debate. Violence or threats are involved in only a minority of such offenses. Offenders may genuinely believe that the "victim" is of age, and young persons may be guilty of encouraging or even of enticing offenders. In addition, some psychologists argue that sexual offenses generally affect children much less than many parents believe. Despite all these arguments, few people would like to see a society in which psychologically and physically immature individuals have no legal protection

**Types of sex offense**
A US study (Gebhard et al) found the following distribution of offenses among 1021 imprisoned offenders with victims under 15.
**1** Heterosexual offenses (no force or threats used) **46%.**
**2** Homosexual offenses **31%.**
**3** Incest (daughter or step-) **14%.**
**4** Heterosexual aggressions (force or threats used) **6%.**
**5** Miscellaneous offenses **3%.**

against sexual experiences with which they are ill-fitted to cope. Pedophiles — adults who derive erotic pleasure from relationships with children — may deserve a more sympathetic hearing, but they seem unlikely to win much popular support. In incest cases, condemnation of adult-child sexual relations is reinforced by a further deeply rooted taboo. In cases involving coitus with a willing partner under the legal age of consent — termed statutory rape in the USA — sympathy is greater when the offender is young and where there could be reasonable doubt as to the age of the partner.

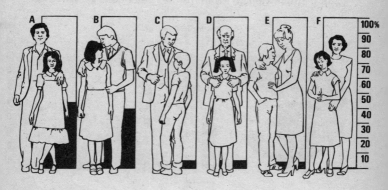

**Incest offenders**
This diagram, based on a German study (H. Maisch) of 78 adult-minor incest cases, shows percentages involving different family relationships.
**A** Father-daughter 44%.
**B** Stepfather-stepdaughter 41%.
**C** Father-son 5%.
**D** Grandfather-granddaughter 5%.
**E** Mother-son 4%.
**F** Mother-daughter 1%.

© DIAGRAM

# Other sex offenses

A further group of sex offenses can be considered under the heading of "public nuisance" offenses. The offenders typically have no wish to harm their victims, but seek sexual gratification in ways that are offensive or disturbing to others. Most significant in terms of numbers of persons convicted are exhibitionists (see pp. 316-317), mainly because the nature of their offense makes them most likely to be detected and reported. Peepers (see pp. 318-319) are probably more numerous than arrests would suggest, and persons making obscene telephone calls are generally unlikely to be traced. Frotteurs and toucheurs — individuals

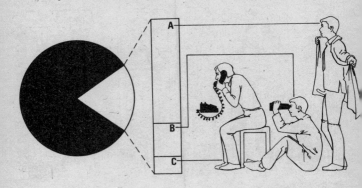

**Nuisance offenses**
Based on a US study of 2234 sex offenses by imprisoned sex offenders (Gebhard, Gagnon, Pomeroy, Christenson), this diagram shows how nearly 20% of the total were accounted for by three types of "public nuisance" offense.
A Exhibitionism 13%.
B Peeping 4%.
C Obscene communicating 2%.

who stroke or touch others in a sexually provocative manner — are typically not reported despite the annoyance caused. Finally we look at three very different crimes against consensual morality. Necrophilia — sexual relations with the dead — is a rare crime sometimes found with homicide. Bestiality — relations with animals — may be fairly common in country districts but is not often detected. Incestuous relations between consenting adults continue to be generally condemned when a close blood relationship is involved, but there is a tendency toward greater liberality when the relationship is one through marriage.

**Exhibitionism offenses**
A study (Ellis and Brancale) of the offenses committed by 89 exhibitionists in a New Jersey diagnostic center produced the following breakdown of types.
**1** Exhibiting genitals to adult females 40%.
**2** Exhibiting genitals to minor females 28%.
**3** Masturbating in public 22%.
**4** "Indecent exposure" 9%.

# Further reading

**General books**

Ardener S. (Ed.) *Defining Females* Croom Helm, 1978

Armytage W.H.G., Chester R., Peel J. (Eds.) *Changing Patterns of Sexual Behaviour* Academic Press, 1980

Begley D.J., Firth J.A., Hoult J.R.S. *Human Reproduction and Developmental Biology* Macmillan, 1980

Berne E. *Sex in Human Loving* André Deutsch, 1971

Brecher R., Brecher E. (Eds.) *An Analysis of Human Sexual Response* New American Library, 1966

British Medical Journal *Aspects of Sexual Medicine* BMA, 1976

Broderick C.B., Bernard J. *The Individual, Sex, and Society* Johns Hopkins Press, 1969

Cohn F. *Understanding Human Sexuality* Prentice-Hall, 1974

Comfort A. *The Joy of Sex* Quartet Books, 1974

Cook M., McHenry R. *Sexual Attraction* Pergamon Press, 1978

Cook M., Wilson G. (Eds.) *Love and Attraction* Pergamon Press, 1979

Diagram Group *Man's Body* Paddington Press, 1976

Diagram Group *Woman's Body* Paddington Press, 1977

Ellis A., Abarbanel A. *The Encyclopedia of Sexual Behavior* Hawthorn Books, 1961

Eysenck H.J. *Sex and Personality* Open Books, 1976

Eysenck H.J., Wilson G. *The Psychology of Sex* J.M. Dent & Sons, 1979

Feldman P., MacCulloch M. *Human Sexual Behavior* John Wiley & Sons, 1980

Fisher S. *The Female Orgasm* Basic Books, 1973

Ford C.S., Beach F.A. *Patterns of Sexual Behavior* Harper & Row, 1951

Freud S. *On Sexuality* Penguin Books, 1977

Gagnon J.H., Simon W. *Sexual Conduct* Hutchinson, 1974

Green R. *Sexual Identity Conflict in Children and Adults* Duckworth, 1974

Hite S. *The Hite Report* Dell Publishing Company, 1976

Katchadourian H.A., Lunde D.T. *Fundamentals of Human Sexuality* Holt, Reinhart & Winston, 2nd ed. 1975

Kelly G.F. *Sexuality: The Human Perspective* Barron's Educational, 1980

Kinsey A.C., et al. *Sexual Behavior in the Human Female* W.B. Saunders, 1953

Kinsey A.C., et al. *Sexual Behavior in the Human Male* W.B. Saunders, 1948

Kogan B.A. *Human Sexual Expression* Harcourt Brace Jovanovich, 1970

Legman G. *Oral Techniques in Sexual Intercourse* Duckworth, 1974

Lloyd B., Archer J. (Eds.) *Exploring Sex Differences* Academic Press, 1976

Masters W.H., Johnson V.E. *Human Sexual Response* Little, Brown & Company, 1966

McCary J.L. *Human Sexuality* D. Van Nostrand, 3rd ed. 1978

McCary J.L. *Sexual Myths and Fallacies* Van Nostrand Reinhold, 1971

Pengelly E.T. *Sex and Human Life* Addison, 1974

Pietropinto A., Simenauer J. *Beyond the Male Myth* Times Books, 1977

Reed E. *Woman's Evolution* Pathfinder Press, 1975

Reik T. *Psychology of Sex Relations* Grove, 1966

Sadock B.J., Kaplan H.L., Freedman A.M. *The Sexual Experience* Williams & Wilkins, 1976

Schofield M. *The Sexual Behaviour of Young Adults* Allen Lane, 1973

Schofield M. *The Sexual Behaviour of Young People* Longmans Green, 1965

Semmons J.P., Krantz K.E. *The Adolescent Experience* Macmillan, 1970

Smith M.S. *Sex and Society* Hodder & Stoughton, 1975

Sorensen R.C. *Adolescent Sexuality in Contemporary America* World Publishing Company, 1973

Tannahill R. *Sex in History* Hamish Hamilton, 1980

Thomson B., Collard J. *Who Divorces?* Routledge & Kegan Paul, 1979

Wagner N.N. *Perspectives on Human Sexuality* Behavioral Publications, 1974

Weinberg M.S. *Sex Research: Studies from the Kinsey Institute* Oxford University Press, 1976

Wilson G., Nais D. *Love's Mysteries: The Psychology of Sexual Attraction* Open Books, 1976

**Birth control**

Farrell C., Kellaher L. *My Mother Said: The Way Young People Learned About Sex and Birth Control* Routledge & Kegan Paul, 1978

Hatcher R.A. (Ed.) *Contraceptive Technology 1980-81* Irvington, 1980

Potts M., Bhiwandiwala P. (Eds.) *Birth Control: An International Assessment* MTP Press, 1979

Ramaswamy S., Smith T. *Practical Contraception* Pitman Medical, 1976

Shapiro H.I. *The Birth Control Book* St. Martin's Press, 1977

**Infertility**

Harrison M. *Infertility: A Guide for Couples* Houghton Mifflin Company, 1979

Kleinman R.L., Senanayake P. (Eds.) *Handbook on Infertility* IPPF, 1979

Menning B.E. *Infertility: A Guide for the Childless Couple* Prentice-Hall, 1977

Stangel J.J. *Fertility and Conception* Paddington Press, 1979

**Aging and sex**

Bowskill D., Linacre A. *The "Male" Menopause* Frederick Muller, 1976

Bromley D.B. *The Psychology of Human Ageing* Penguin Books 1966, 1974

Butler R.N., Lewis M. *Sex After Sixty* George Prior Publishers, 1976

Conran S. *Futures* Sidgwick & Jackson, 1979

Felstein I. *Sex in Later Life* Granada, 1980

Nudel A. *For the Woman Over Fifty* Avon Books, 1978

### Sexual problems

Belliveau F., Richter L. *Understanding Human Sexual Inadequacy* Little, Brown & Company, 1970

Crown S. (Ed.) *Psychosexual Problems: Psychotherapy, Counseling and Behavioral Modification* Grune & Stratton, 1976

Kaplan H.S. *The New Sex Therapy* Penguin Books, 1974

Masters W.H., Johnson V.E. *Human Sexual Inadequacy* Churchill, 1970

Trimmer E. *Basic Sexual Medicine* William Heinemann Medical Books, 1978

### Sexual infections

Barlow D. *Sexually Transmitted Diseases: The Facts* Oxford University Press, 1979

Llewellyn-Jones D. *Sex and V.D.* Faber and Faber, 1974

Noble R.C. *Sexually Transmitted Diseases* Henry Kimpton, 1979

Oates J.K. *Sexually Transmitted Diseases* Women's Health Concern, 1979

Schofield C.B.S. *Sexually Transmitted Diseases* Churchill Livingstone, 3rd ed. 1979

### Homosexuality

Bell A.P., Weinberg M.S. *Homosexualities: A Study of Diversity among Men and Women* Touchstone, 1978

Ettorre E.M. *Lesbians, Women and Society* Routledge & Kegan Paul, 1980

Masters W.H., Johnson V.E. *Homosexuality in Perspective* Little, Brown & Company, 1979

Spada J. *The Spada Report* New American Library, 1979

West D.J. *Homosexuality Re-examined* Gerald Duckworth, 1977

Wolff D. *Bisexuality: A Study* Quartet Books, 2nd ed. 1979

### Unconventional sex

Ellis A. *The Civilized Couple's Guide to Extramarital Adventure* Wyden, 1972

Gosselin C., Wilson G. *Sexual Variations: Fetishism, Transvestism and Sado-masochism* Faber and Faber, 1980

Reik T. *Masochism in Modern Man* Grove Press, 1957

Stoller R. *Perversion: The Erotic Form of Hatred* Delta, 1975

Stoller R. *Sex and Gender: The Transsexual Experiment* The Hogarth Press, 1975

Storr A. *Sexual Deviation* Penguin Books, 1964

### Sex and crime

Amir M. *Patterns in Forcible Rape* University of Chicago Press, 1971

Chappell D., Geis R., Geis G. (Eds.) *Forcible Rape: The Crime, the Victim and the Offender* Columbia University Press, 1977

Gebhard P.H. et al. *Sex Offenders: An Analysis of Types* Harper Row, 1965

MacNamara D.E.J., Sagarin E. *Sex, Crime and the Law* The Free Press, 1977

Maisch H. *Incest* André Deutsch, 1973

# Index